SPARKNOTES

Power Tactics

FOR THE NEW SAT

THE CRITICAL READING SECTION
READING PASSAGES

SPARK
NOTES

A DIVISION OF BARNES & NOBLE PUBLISHING

SPARKNOTES is a registered trademark of SparkNotes LLC

Spark Educational Publishing
A Division of Barnes & Noble Publishing
120 Fifth Avenue
New York, NY 10011

ISBN 1-4114-0272-3

Please submit changes or report errors to *www.sparknotes.com/errors*

Printed and bound in Canada.

SAT is the registered trademark of the College Entrance Examination Board, which was not involved in the production of, and does not endorse, this product.

Written by Doug Tarnopol

CONTENTS

INTRODUCTION

Truly effective SAT preparation doesn't need to be painful or time-consuming. SparkNotes' *Power Tactics for the New SAT* is proof that powerful test preparation can be streamlined so that you study only what you need. Instead of toiling away through a 700-page book or an expensive six-week course, you can choose the *Power Tactics* book that gets you where you want to be a lot sooner.

Perhaps you're Kid Math, the fastest number-slinger this side of the Mississippi, but a bit of a bumbler when it comes to words. Or maybe you've got the verbal parts down but can't seem to manage algebraic functions. *Power Tactics for the New SAT* provides an extremely focused review of every component on the new SAT, so you can design your own program of study.

If you're not exactly sure where you fall short, log on to **testprep.sparknotes.com/powertactics** and take our free diagnostic SAT test. This test will pinpoint your weaknesses and reveal exactly where to focus.

Since you're holding this book in your hands, it's pretty likely that Reading Passages are giving you trouble. You've made the right decision because in a few short hours, you will have mastered this part of the exam. No sweat, no major investment of time or money, no problem.

So, let's not waste any time: go forth and conquer Reading Passages so you can get on with the *better parts* of your life!

ABOUT THE NEW SAT

THE OLD

The SAT, first administered in 1926, has undergone a thorough restructuring. For the last ten years, the SAT consisted of two sections: Verbal and Math. The Verbal section contained Analogies, Sentence Completions, and Critical Reading passages and questions. The Math section tested arithmetic, algebra, and geometry, as well as some probability, statistics, and data interpretation.

You received one point for each correct answer. For most questions, a quarter of a point was deducted for each incorrect answer. This was called the "wrong-answer penalty," which was designed to neutralize random guessing. If you simply filled in the bubble sheet at random, you'd likely get one-fifth of the items correct, given that each item has five answer choices (excluding student-produced–response items). You'd also get four-fifths of the items wrong, losing $4 \times {}^1/4$, or 1 point for the four incorrectly answered items. Every time you determined an answer choice was wrong, you'd improve your odds by beating the wrong-answer penalty. The net number of points (less wrong-answer penalties) was called the "raw score."

Raw score = # of correct answers – (${}^1/4$ × # of wrong answers)

That score was then converted to the familiar 200–800 "scaled score."

THE NEW

For 2005, the SAT added a Writing section and an essay, changed the name of *Verbal* to *Critical Reading*, and added algebra II content to the Math section. The following chart compares the old SAT with the new SAT:

Old SAT	New SAT
Verbal	**Critical Reading**
Analogies	*Eliminated*
Sentence Completions	Sentence Completions
Long Reading Passages	Long Reading Passages
Paired Reading Passages	Paired Reading Passages
	Short Reading Passages
Math—Question Types	
Multiple Choice	Multiple Choice
Quantitative Comparisons	*Eliminated*
Student-produced Responses	Student-produced Responses
Math—Content Areas	
Numbers & Operations	Numbers & Operations
Algebra I	Algebra I
	Algebra II
Geometry	Geometry
Data Analysis, Statistics & Probability	Data Analysis, Statistics & Probability
	Writing
	Identifying Sentence Errors
	Improving Sentences
	Improving Paragraphs
	Essay
Total Time: 3 hours	*Total Time*: 3 hours, 45 minutes
Maximum Scaled Score: 1600	*Maximum Scaled Score*: 2400 Separate Essay Score (2–12)

The scoring for the test is the same, except that the Writing section provides a third 200–800 scaled score, and there is now a separate essay score. The wrong-answer penalty is still in effect.

NEW PACKAGE, OLD PRODUCT

While the test has changed for test-*takers*, it has not changed all that much from the test-*maker*'s point of view. The Educational Testing Service (ETS) is a not-for-profit institute that creates the SAT for The College Board. Test creation is not as simple a task as you might think. Any standardized test question has to go through a rigorous series of editorial reviews and statistical studies before it can be released to the public. In fact, that's why the old SAT featured a seventh unscored, "experimental" section: new questions were introduced and tested out in these sections. ETS "feeds" potential questions to its test-takers to measure the level of difficulty. Given the complex and lengthy process of developing new questions, it would be impossible for ETS to introduce *totally* new question types or make major changes to existing question types.

Now that you know these facts, the "new" SAT will start to make more sense. The changes were neither random nor unexpected. Actually, the only truly *new* question type on the SAT is the short reading passage followed by a couple of questions. However, the skills tested and strategies required are virtually identical to the tried-and-true long reading-passage question type. All other additions to the test consist of new *content*, rather than new *question types*. Both multiple-choice and student-produced–response math questions ("grid-ins") will now feature algebra II concepts. Same question type, new content. Critical Reading features one fiction passage per test, as well as questions on genre, rhetorical devices, and cause and effect. Same question type, different content.

Even the much-feared new Writing Section is in a sense old news. The PSAT and the SAT II Writing test have featured exactly the same multiple-choice question types for years. The essay format and scoring rubric are virtually identical to those of the SAT II Writing test. The College Board had no other choice, given how long the test-development process is.

The other major changes are omissions, not additions: Quantitative Comparisons and Analogies have been dumped from the test.

So, in a nutshell, ETS has simply attached an SAT II Writing test to the old SAT, dropped Analogies and Quantitative Comparisons, added some algebra II content and short reading passages, and ensured that some fiction and fiction-related questions are included. That's it.

A USER'S GUIDE

Reading this book will maximize your score on Reading Passages. We've divided up your study of Reading Passages into two sections: **Power Tactics** and **Practice Sets**. The Power Tactics will provide you with important concepts and strategies you'll need to tackle Reading Passages. The Practice Sets will give you an opportunity to apply what you learn to SAT questions. To achieve your target score, you'll learn:

- The major passage and question types you'll encounter in **Short Passages**, **Long Passages**, and **Paired Passages**.
- What the test-makers are actually trying to test with SAT Reading Passages.
- Essential concepts and powerful step methods to maximize your score.
- The art of *skimming*
- Test-taking strategies that allow you to approach each question with the best possible mindset.
- The 11 most common mistakes and how to avoid them.

In order to get the most out of this book:

- Make sure to read each section thoroughly and carefully.
- Don't skip the Guided Practice questions!
- Read all explanations to all questions.
- Go to **testprep.sparknotes.com/powertactics** for a free full-length diagnostic **pretest**. The test will help you determine your strengths and weaknesses for Reading Passages and for the entire SAT.
- Go back to our website after you complete this book to take a **posttest**. This test tells you how well you've mastered Reading Passages and what topics you still need to review.

Look upon this book as your personal trainer. If you stick with the training program, you'll reach your full potential.

THE POWER
TACTICS

ANATOMY OF THE SAT READING PASSAGE

There are three types of Reading Passages (RPs) on the new SAT:

- The Long RP
- The Short RP
- The Paired RP

Let's take a look at an example of an RP. We mean "look" literally: please don't bother reading the passage now!

THE LONG RP

The purpose of this example is merely to give you an idea of what an RP *looks* like and to introduce the terms we'll be using to refer to the various parts of an SAT RP. We'll be returning to this RP throughout this book, so you'll have ample opportunity to work through it.

Directions: The passage below is followed by questions based on the content of the passage. Answer the questions on the basis of what the passage **states** or **implies** and on any introductory material provided.

The following passage is taken from an article on the architecture of the Etruscans, a tribe that dominated Italy before the rise of the Romans, and the Roman architect Vitruvius' On Architecture, *which was written in the first century B.C. during the reign of the emperor Augustus.*

As we have seen, decades of archeological research have shown that
Vitruvius' famous chapter on Etruscan temples idealized readily
apparent diversity. While Vitruvius did accurately capture the main
features of the Etruscan style, actual Etruscan temples deviated quite
significantly from his ideal. We might ask why Vitruvius ignored the
architectural diversity of the many different Etruscan temples with
which he clearly was familiar. Answering this question provides some
useful insight into not only Vitruvius' definition of the Etruscan style
but also the purpose of *On Architecture* as a whole.

Traditionally, scholars answered this question by pointing to
Vitruvius' allegiance to Greek philosophy. In chapter six, Vitruvius
reports that he has had the benefit of a liberal Greek education, which
he recommends to all aspiring architects. Without such broad training,
Vitruvius argues, no architect can understand proper architectural
theory. For Vitruvius, architectural theory rested on the principles of
mathematical proportion promulgated by such Greek philosophers as
Pythagoras. These philosophers believed that the universe was
structured according to god-given mathematical laws. They further
believed that the harmonious mathematical structure of the universe
(the *macrocosm*) was reflected in the structure of the human body (the
microcosm). Vitruvius extended this reflection to architectural forms.
Temples, Vitruvius believed, must reflect the mathematical
proportionality of the body, just as the body reflects the mathematical
proportionality of the universe. Thus, Vitruvius claimed to "find"
correspondences between proportional measurements of the human
body—that the hand's length is one-tenth the body's height, for
example—and proportional measurements of the Etruscan temple.
Vitruvius Hellenized the Etruscan temple by superimposing Greek
notions of mathematical proportionality on his purportedly empirical
description of the Etruscan temple style.

Vitruvius' belief that specific natural proportions should be extended
to architectural forms does help to explain why he idealized Etruscan
temples. After all, mathematical models generally don't allow for much
deviation. However, far more mundane considerations acted in concert
with Vitruvius' allegiance to Greek notions of mathematical harmony to
encourage the idealization of the Etruscan temple.

13

Despite its title, *On Architecture* was not written primarily for architects. It was written to convince the emperor Augustus, the most powerful patron in Rome, to give Vitruvius the opportunity to do large-scale architectural work. Vitruvius knew that if Augustus devoted any time at all to *On Architecture*, the emperor would most likely do what busy executives still do to this day: he would read the introductions to each of the ten chapters and skip the rest of the book. Reading *On Architecture* in this manner—each introduction in sequence—is a revelation. One quickly realizes that the chapter introductions constitute an ancient résumé designed to convince Augustus to entrust part of his architectural legacy to Vitruvius.

Moreover, one must also keep in mind that *On Architecture*, like all ancient books, was originally published as a series of scrolls. Each modern "chapter" most likely corresponds to one ancient scroll. This physical form lent even greater significance to the snappy, pertinent introductions and the concise writing that modern readers also demand. The physical act of reading a scroll made the kind of flipping back and forth that modern paginated books allow significantly more inconvenient. Scrolls strongly encouraged ancient authors to front-load the most important ideas they wanted to convey. The ancient author had to earn each "unrolling" by concentrating that much more on the order in which ideas were presented and the economy with which they were expressed—and how much more so when one's intended audience is the emperor of Rome?

Vitruvius' idealization of Etruscan temples now becomes even more understandable. Tellingly, Vitruvius buried his discussion of Etruscan temples toward the end of a chapter (i.e., scroll), which reveals that Vitruvius considered Etruscan temples to be relatively unimportant. In the unlikely event that Augustus (or his appointed reader) might have actually put in the effort to reach this discussion, the last thing Vitruvius would have wanted his exalted audience to encounter is any unnecessary detail. In order to capture Augustus' attention—and patronage—Vitruvius had to demonstrate his complete command of architecture in the smallest, most easily digestible package possible. The purpose of *On Architecture* was not to record architectural variety in encyclopedic detail but rather to gain architectural commissions. This fact, along with Vitruvius' fundamental belief in proportionality, goes a long way toward explaining why Vitruvius ignored the architectural diversity he doubtless saw in Etruscan temples.

1. As used in line 12, the word "liberal" most nearly means

(A) tolerant
(B) generous
(C) free-thinking
(D) wide-ranging
(E) narrow

2. On the whole, the author's attitude toward the traditional scholarly explanation of Vitruvius' description of the Etruscan temple style described in lines 10–30 is one of

(A) indifference
(B) respect
(C) frustration
(D) interest
(E) mistrust

3. The principal function of the fifth paragraph (lines 48–60) is to show

(A) that contemporary architects did not find *On Architecture* helpful to their work
(B) why Vitruvius ended up building so many structures for Augustus
(D) how Vitruvius constructed *On Architecture*'s ten chapters with his audience's likely reading habits in mind that Augustus was as busy as any modern-day executive
(E) how the nature of ancient scrolls discouraged readers

4. The author would most likely agree that the physical form of ancient books

(A) prevented ancient authors from writing as well as modern authors
(B) encouraged the writing of encyclopedic overviews
(C) was responsible for the spread of ancient knowledge
(D) is a unique source of insight into ancient writing largely ignored by traditional scholars
(E) undermined the ability of ancient authors to gain patrons

5.   The main purpose of the passage is to

(A)   expose Vitruvius' dishonesty

(B)   prove the value of a Greek education

(C)   suggest that Vitruvius considered Etruscan temples to be the most important type of temple

(D)   discuss the differences between ancient scrolls and modern books

(E)   account for the difference between Vitruvius' written description of Etruscan temples and their archaeological remains

This RP may look pretty intimidating, but this is precisely what a real RP on the SAT is like. We're here to give you detailed, focused preparation, and the best way to achieve that is by throwing you in the deep end of the pool. If you follow the concepts and strategies in this book, *and* if you give yourself plenty of time to practice, you'll be acing RPs like this one in no time at all.

As you can see, a long RP consists of boxed **directions**, an italicized **introduction**, a multiparagraph **passage**, and several **items**, which is the more formal term for "questions." Each item consists of a **stem** and five **answer choices**. One of these answer choices is correct; the other four answer choices are called **distractors** because they are designed to *distract* attention from the correct answer choice. The entire unit of passage-plus-items is called a **set**. Line numbers are given in the left-hand margin, as shown.

Long passages contain roughly 400 to 800 words, but this number has varied on past SATs, so you might see somewhat shorter or somewhat longer passages. As you'll soon learn, the actual length of a passage doesn't have a direct impact on how you handle reading passage sets.

THE SHORT RP AND THE PAIRED RP

There are two other types of passage sets: Short RPs and Paired RPs. They share all the characteristics of a Long RP with the following exceptions:

- Short RPs are one or two paragraphs long, and around 100 to 200 words. They only have a couple of items each. Short RP sets are really just scaled-down long RP sets. There's nothing particularly unique about them; if anything, the prose in the passage seems to be a little easier to understand than that of a long RP. Short RPs are a new feature of the SAT.

- Paired RPs consist of two passages and a set of items. Both passages discuss the same topic or theme, but each one takes a different position on the subject matter. The first few items in the set are based on Passage 1; the next few items are based on Passage 2; the last few items are based on both passages. Each passage is around 250 to 600 words long. You will see at least one paired passage set. You may see paired *short* RPs as well, which contain fewer paragraphs, words, and items.

In this book, we use a long RP set to teach the step methods you'll need to maximize your score. Where appropriate, we point out the minor differences in method that these "special-case" passage sets require. You'll have ample opportunity to practice short and paired RPs in the practice sets at the end of this book.

WHAT SAT RPS TEST

RPs test specific reading skills needed to make sense of paragraphs and longer chunks of prose. You'll be expected to:

- Recognize the major features of an RP: **topic, main idea, purpose, tone, theme, and logic**.
- Recognize the use of rhetorical devices and literary techniques, including: **hyperbole, repetition, imagery and figurative language, sound patterns, rhetorical questions, idioms and clichés, irony, foreshadowing, and motif**.
- Decode unfamiliar words from context.
- Find informational details (facts) in the passage.
- Identify cause and effect and follow the logic of arguments.
- Compare and contrast arguments.

Don't worry if some of these terms look unfamiliar or confusing: we'll cover everything in the following sections.

Passages can be either nonfiction or fiction. Nonfiction passages can be on any topic in one of three broad areas: science, social science, and the humanities. Items are never based on outside knowledge; all the information you need to answer the items is in the passage. Passages may feature a couple of unfamiliar terms related to the topic at hand, but these terms are always defined within the passage.

A major change to the new SAT is the addition of fiction passages. The good news is that pre–2005 SATs have featured fiction passages on occasion, so we have a good idea what these RPs look like. The fictional prose you will see will be straightforward and conventional and most likely concerned with issues of personal development or family relationships. Standardized tests tend to stay away from controversial topics such as war, sex, death, or politics. While some familiarity with basic literary techniques is required, the fiction sets are pretty similar to the old-style nonfiction sets.

Before we can jump into the methods you'll use to handle RPs, there are a few essential concepts and skills you'll need to get under your belt. Let's take a look at those now.

ESSENTIAL CONCEPTS

Before you tackle RP passages, items, and sets, you'll need to be familiar with a few distinct concepts. Mountains of books have been written on the topics below; we've whittled them down to their essential SAT-related core. We've also played a little fast and loose with some concepts and names for the greater good of simplicity and usability.

RP concepts are not as discrete as mathematical concepts. Many of them blend into and depend upon one another. Don't let this discourage you: the main point is just to become familiar with these concepts.

MAJOR FEATURES OF AN RP

Topic

The **topic** is the subject matter treated in a passage. This may seem obvious, but there's a bit of a twist, as you'll soon see. Read the passage below and write down what you think the topic is in the space provided:

Giuseppe Verdi secured his place in history by dominating the Italian opera scene for almost fifty years. The middle and late decades of the nineteenth century were Verdi's most productive years. During this period, Italy transitioned from a collection of small states, several of which were controlled by foreign powers, to a unified and independent nation. It is no surprise, therefore, that many of Verdi's operas center on themes of political struggle, oppression, and liberation.

Today, Verdi is most appreciated for the passion expressed in his arias, the name given to the points in the operas where one character, often the lead, gives a solo performance accompanied only by the orchestra. Historians, however, should recognize that Verdi's greatest gift to the world was his commentary on a particularly turbulent period in the development of modern Europe's political scene.

Your answer	
Our answer	The themes of Verdi's operas

Scope

The topic is not necessarily so straightforward in an RP. In order to correctly identify the topic, you need to consider a passage's **scope**. A correctly identified topic has the appropriate scope—neither too broad nor too narrow. Think of scope as the breadth of the topic covered in the passage. In the passage above, the topic is the themes of Verdi's operas. The chart below shows different ways of being outside the scope of this passage.

Example of topic's scope	Description of scope
European music	way, way too broad
nineteenth-century European music	way too broad
Verdi's music	too broad
the themes of Verdi's operas	just right
the themes of Verdi's arias	too narrow
the passion in Verdi's arias	way too narrow
the passion in one character's aria in a Verdi opera	way, way too narrow
nineteenth-century Italian politics	off topic

Note how scope can be either too broad, too narrow, or just plain off-topic. One way to think of scope is to compare it to the frame of a photograph. If you want to photograph, say, your house, you'll certainly want something in between a satellite photo of the entire Earth and an electron micrograph of the wood on your front door! You'll want just the front of the house with a little space on all sides to show a bit of the yard and trees. And you don't want a picture of someone else's house or of, say, the White House or the Empire State Building. That would be "off topic," so to speak.

Search Engines

Another way to think of topic and scope is to pretend that you're categorizing the passage for retrieval by an internet search engine. You want to get the minimum number of "hits" or "matches" without choosing a scope so small that your search will miss the article completely. The Verdi passage could be categorized under "European music," but that would cover two thousand years of all types of popular and classical music for the entire continent. "Nineteenth-century European music" is more specific, but still includes every type of music from every European country. "Verdi's music" is getting closer, but still doesn't focus specifically on his operas. And the excessively narrow scopes focus on certain aspects of Verdi's operas—the arias—that are mentioned but that are not the proper scope of the passage. Finally, "nineteenth-century Italian politics" is also mentioned, but we're concerned with the relationship between Verdi's operatic themes and nineteenth-century Italian politics, not with nineteenth-century Italian politics in and of itself.

Therefore, if you had to choose a categorization for a search engine that would retrieve this passage as quickly as possible, it would be the underlined one below.

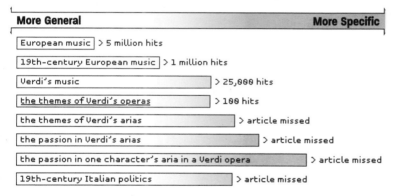

More General		**More Specific**
European music	> 5 million hits	
19th-century European music	> 1 million hits	
Verdi's music	> 25,000 hits	
the themes of Verdi's operas	> 100 hits	
the themes of Verdi's arias	> article missed	
the passion in Verdi's arias	> article missed	
the passion in one character's aria in a Verdi opera	> article missed	
19th-century Italian politics	> article missed	

Main Idea

The **main idea** of a passage is the central point that the author is making. Go back to the Verdi passage again: write down what you think the main idea of this passage is in the space below. Then, read our answer.

Your answer	
Our answer	The themes of Verdi's operas are concerned with the political turmoil of nineteenth-century Italy.

A text's main idea encompasses more than the details—it's the one phrase or sentence that covers the topic. Think of it this way: in a dresser drawer, you keep your socks, your underwear, and your t-shirts. The "main idea" of that drawer is not "socks" or "underwear" or "t-shirts"— it's "undergarments."

Therefore, the main idea is a clear expression of the topic and scope, along with the author's particular take on that topic and scope. Here's a comparison of the topic and main idea for the passage we've been using:

Topic	The themes of Verdi's operas
Main Idea	The themes of Verdi's operas are concerned with the political turmoil of nineteenth-century Italy.

You'll usually find one main idea item per long or paired RP.

Purpose

Purpose refers to the *author's* purpose. Why did he or she write this passage? What is the point he or she is trying to make? Take the Verdi example again: write the author's purpose in the space provided below.

Your answer	
Our answer	The author's purpose is to argue that Verdi should be most appreciated for the political commentary in his operas, not for the passion expressed in his opera's famous arias.

Whereas the main idea tells you *what* the author wrote, the purpose tells you *why*. Virtually all nonfiction passages contain an argument—an assertion backed up by evidence. (We'll go over these terms shortly.) Even fiction passages contain purpose. An author can write fiction on any topic; what an author chooses to write about exposes the author's purpose. If, for example, an author writes sympathetically about the hard times poor American farmers faced in the Great Depression, that author's purpose is likely to raise awareness of the plight and dignity of those farmers and their families.

The following chart compares topic, main idea, and purpose for the passage we've been using.

Topic	The themes of Verdi's operas
Main Idea	The themes of Verdi's operas are concerned with the political turmoil of nineteenth-century Italy.
Purpose	To argue that Verdi should be most appreciated for the political commentary in his operas, not for the passion expressed in his opera's famous arias.

Tone

Tone is often a difficult concept to grasp. It's based both on a passage's style and on the particular words used in the passage. The way an author uses language implies how the author was feeling at the time. Was she angry? Sad? Excited? Resigned? Depressed?

Read the Verdi passage once more, looking for clues about the passage's tone. Then, write a description of the tone in the space provided below.

Your answer	
Our answer	·ʇuǝɯnƃɹɐ pǝuosɐǝɹ ɟo ǝuo sı ǝuoʇ ǝɥ⊥

The author acknowledges that Verdi's arias have garnered the most praise but argues that the political commentary is more impressive and important. What's the tone of the following passage?

Giuseppe Verdi would not appreciate the place in history our blinkered historians have given him. Dominating the Italian opera scene for almost fifty years, Verdi's most productive period was the middle and late decades of the nineteenth century. During this period, Italy transitioned from a collection of small states, several of which were controlled by foreign powers, to a unified and independent nation.

From a perusal of their writings on Verdi, one would think that most esteemed contemporary music historians are blissfully unaware of this fact. Of course they know about Verdi's historical context, but these genteel commentators apparently still cling naively to the notion that art is created by transcendent geniuses. It is no surprise, therefore, that these historians ignore the messy political context in which Verdi composed and concentrate on technical matters of musical composition—as though the two could ever be separated. That Verdi's operas center on themes of political struggle, oppression, and liberation is merely window dressing to these writers and thus not crucial to understanding Verdi's music.

Today, Verdi is most likely to be appreciated for the passion expressed in his arias, the name given to the points in the operas where one character, often the lead, gives a solo performance accompanied only by the orchestra. Historians, however, should deepen the public's appreciation of Verdi by recognizing that Verdi's greatest gift to the world was his commentary on a particularly turbulent period in the development of modern Europe's political scene.

The tone is much harsher and more combative, isn't it? This author is obviously a lot more annoyed by the current basis for Verdi's fame. The two passages share the same topic, scope, and main idea. But the tone is radically different. The first passage had a relaxed tone; the author was suggesting another and better way to appreciate Verdi's operas. The second passage is much angrier and more sarcastic. The author is ridiculing the ignorance of contemporary historians rather than merely suggesting an alternative viewpoint.

Theme

Theme is another difficult concept to grasp. Like the main idea, the theme can be described as the passage's subject matter, but themes are usually deeper and more general than main ideas.

For example, here's what we've already determined about the Verdi passage:

Topic	The themes of Verdi's operas
Main Idea	The themes of Verdi's operas are concerned with the political turmoil of nineteenth-century Italy.

Purpose	To argue that Verdi should be most appreciated for the political commentary in his operas, not for the passion expressed in his opera's famous arias.
Tone	Reasoned argument

What theme does the author touch upon? One way of putting it is:

The historical subject matter of opera should be as much the basis for appreciation as the beauty of the music itself.

Themes are also important in fiction, because they allow readers to look for deeper meaning in a story. The chart below provides some plots or subject matter along with some classic themes. The point is not to memorize these themes, but to use this chart to begin to understand the difference between topic, main idea, and theme.

Plot/Subject Matter	Theme
A man is killed in a forest. Several witnesses give their version of what happened. Each story is different; many contradict one another.	The subjectivity of human knowledge
A media mogul dies. His life is reviewed by his friends and enemies. They cannot figure out why he did many of the things that he did, but the audience finds out that he never got over being separated from his mother as a young boy.	Loss of innocence
Two historians are arguing over the importance of Julius Caesar. One historian claims that Caesar single-handedly reshaped Roman civilization. The other historian claims that Caesar was a reflection of his time and place, and that if Caesar had not arisen and changed Roman history, someone else would have done so in much the same way. Thus, Caesar didn't make history; he merely embodied the spirit of his age.	Free will vs. predetermination in human actions
A soldier returning from war is delayed on his trip home. He goes through many trials and tribulations before finally reaching his home.	The journey

Themes don't have to be as grandiose as the ones listed in the chart. They can be as mundane as proverbs. For example, the theme of this book is: the more you understand the structure and content of RPs, the more likely you are to maximize your potential on that part of the SAT.

Logic

Logic is as important in fiction as it is in nonfiction. Certain basic rules, such as cause and effect, need to be incorporated to avoid confusion. The argument or plot in an RP will flow logically, and you'll be asked to identify this flow, and perhaps add to it.

Logical flow is most obviously transmitted by **signpost words**, which often link paragraphs. English has many such guide words and phrases. No single SAT test will include them all, but here's a handy list of some common ones:

also	consequently	nevertheless	still
although	despite	no less than	therefore
and	even	or	though
as well as	for	otherwise	thus
because	however	since	yet
but	moreover	so	

Sentence structure, too, can show logical flow. How clauses and phrases are positioned and the punctuation used to connect them generates the flow that all good writing must have. We'll point this out in the passage you'll work on later in the book. For now, let's take a look at some key logical terms.

Facts

A **fact** is an objective statement about reality, such as "The Earth is a sphere" or "Charlemagne was a Holy Roman Emperor." Facts can be interpreted in various ways and have various implications.

Fact	Implication or Interpretation
The Earth is a sphere.	I can get from Spain to China by sailing west. Thus, I don't have to only send trading ships east.

Many RP items ask you to find a particular fact in the passage. Other items will ask you to draw out a likely implication from a fact or set of facts; still others will ask you how the author might react to a new fact not in the author's passage.

Assumptions

Assumptions are facts or assertions that are taken for granted and usually unstated. Readers reach conclusions through a combination of facts and assumptions. Identifying underlying assumptions is crucial in RPs.

For example, if an author writes: "The best way to stimulate the economy is by reducing personal income taxes," there are some hidden assumptions to be uncovered. Assumptions aren't *necessarily* true or false, but the SAT wants to ensure that students can identify them.

Statement	Hidden Assumptions
The best way to stimulate the economy is by reducing personal income taxes.	Reducing personal income taxes will actually stimulate the economy.
	The economy needs to be stimulated in the first place.
	Reducing *personal* income taxes, rather than, say, *corporate* income taxes, is a better way to stimulate the economy.
	Reducing *income* taxes, rather than, say, *consumption* taxes (e.g., sales tax) is a better way to stimulate the economy.
	What does *better* mean, anyway? Better for everyone? For most people? In the long run? Right away?

We could go on, but you get the idea. Everyone's writing (and thinking) is littered with hidden assumptions.

Inferences

We *infer* all the time. Here's an example:

Facts	Inference
When I went to sleep last night, there was no snow on the ground.	It snowed while I was asleep.
When I woke up this morning, there was snow on the ground.	

An **inference** is best understood as an unobserved fact that one believes must be true given other observed facts: if there was no snow when I went to bed and there's a ton of snow this morning, you can bet the farm that it snowed overnight.

Some inferences are not as logically necessary as the snow example. They are merely statistically possible or logically probable. For example:

Fact: *Most of the school's students had complained that the dress code was too strict.*

Fact: *The new principal changed the dress code to make it less strict.*

Inference: *Student complaints led to the change in the dress code.*

Well, that *might* be the case. It's plausible—the reasoning used to infer that student complaints led to the policy change makes sense. But there are other possible reasons, each of which is based on a hidden assumption:

Hidden Assumption 1: *The school's administration takes student complaints into account.*

Other Potential Reason: *Parents complained on behalf of their children. The school's administration took these complaints more seriously.*

Hidden Assumption 2: *The new principal changed the policy in response to student complaints rather than out of his own preexisting beliefs.*

Other Potential Reason: *The new principal believes that what students wear doesn't have much of an impact on how they learn.*

Hidden Assumption 3: *The new code reflects student concerns.*

Other Potential Reason: *Maybe the dress code is technically less strict but not in the ways that mattered to the students. For example, let's say that jeans were once banned but are now allowed. That's less strict, but what if 85% of student complaints were about the banning of shorts? Allowing jeans wouldn't address that key complaint.*

Many RP items will ask you to make an inference based on the information given in the passage. You'll need to decide which inferences are valid and which are not. Proper inferences on the SAT tend to be closer to the snow example than to the dress code example—that is, more logically necessary than statistically probable.

RHETORICAL DEVICES AND LITERARY TECHNIQUES

Rhetorical devices and **literary techniques** are closely related to tone and style. In fact, an author's style partly consists of selecting and using certain devices; an author's tone is partially determined by the type of techniques an author uses.

Many SAT books will list lots of Greek terms you don't need to know, such as *synecdoche* and *anaphora*. But the Critical Reading section won't require that you know the *names* of rhetorical devices or literary techniques.

Rather than bombard you with dozens of unfamiliar terms, we'll categorize and clump the most common types of devices and techniques below and provide some examples and commentary. As we said, you won't be specifically tested on these concepts, but they do lurk beneath the surface in the passages. Having a solid understanding of these devices and techniques will improve your ability to handle RPs. Focus on absorbing the similarities and differences between and among them. As you read through the list, note the one key feature all of these techniques and devices share: they allow words and sentences to carry **more** than only their *literal* meaning.

Here is a list of the most important devices and techniques. We've included examples along with commentary on each one:

Hyperbole

I'm as hungry as a starving lion.

Hyperbole is a synonym for *exaggeration*. Clearly, the speaker is not *really* as hungry as a starving lion. A hyperbole is just a figure of speech we use to emphasize a point. The opposite device is **understatement**: *I'm a little tired* is a purposeful understatement if the speaker has been up for 48 hours.

Repetition

Duty does not trump honesty. Duty does not trump common sense. And duty, my friends, does not trump morality.

Repetition is the conscious and purposeful replication of words or phrases in order to make a point. In this example, it's clear that the limits of duty are being sketched out. The speaker is trying to show that duty is not the only or even the most important virtue.

Imagery and Figurative Language

Simile

Her eyes were like stars.

Her eyes are literally human eyes. Figuratively, they are being compared to stars, meaning, most likely, that they are bright and shiny and cause wonderment. This is an example of a **simile**. Similes use *like* and *as* to make explicit comparisons between unlike things, such as eyes and stars.

Metaphor

Her eyes were pools of liquid light.

Again, her eyes are literally human eyes. Figuratively, they are being compared to pools of liquid light. However, the comparison is implied, not stated. This is an example of a **metaphor**. Unlike similes, metaphors compare unlike things without explicitly stating the comparison with "like" or "as."

Personification

Her eyes followed me up the stairs.

Can eyes follow someone up the stairs? Not literally, but in this case an eye—which is not a person—is given a person's abilities, namely, following someone else up the stairs. This is an example of **personification**.

Symbolism

Her eyes looked but did not see. All was dark.

Literally speaking, eyes either see (healthy eyes) or they don't see (blind eyes). An eye that *looks* but does not *see* is blind in a figurative sense. Very often, vision and light are symbols for understanding and en*light*enment. In this example, the woman is most likely unaware of—or "in the dark"—about something. This is an example of **symbolism**.

Sound Patterns

Her eyes were rippling pools of liquid light in which I splashed play-fully.

This metaphor also uses sound patterns to underscore its meaning. Note that the letters *l* and *p* repeat: *ri**pp**ling **p**oo**l**s of **l**iquid **l**ight...s**pl**ashed **pl**ayfully.* The author may have repeated "l" and "p" sounds to evoke the sound of water (like in the word *splash* itself) or simply to link together the words that make up the metaphor—or both. There are many types of sound-pattern devices, each with its own difficult Greek name that you certainly won't need to know.

Rhetorical Questions

Can poverty ever be eradicated?

Rhetorical questions are not meant to be answered. A rhetorical question is used to present what's taken to be an unanswerable question, such as these questions:

Can a repeat offender ever be trusted not to commit another crime?
Can a person ever have too much love?

A rhetorical question can also be one in which the author's answer is clearly intended to be "no" or "yes." In these two examples, the author's answer is clearly intended to be "no" (whether you agree with those answers or not).

Idioms and Clichēs

That'll cost you an arm and a leg.

Idioms are inherited quirks of language that native speakers understand without question but which cause nonnative speakers endless trouble. Only a native speaker knows that if something costs *an arm and a leg* that means it's expensive, not that you actually need to lose your limbs to purchase it. Many overused idioms and symbols are **clichēs**, and clichés themselves can be used ironically (see *irony* below).

Irony

[Said to a mean boss]: "You've been so kind to me."

The SAT *loves* irony. A statement is **ironic** if it expresses something different from or opposite to the literal meaning of the words. This example is called **verbal irony** or **sarcasm**, which can be thought of as "heavy-handed irony":

The overuse of antibiotics has led to the rise of resistant strains of many diseases.

A statement or situation can be ironic or **paradoxical** when the words accurately report events that seem to be contradictory but which have actually occurred, as in this example:

A soldier has returned from a war. He crashes his motorcycle and dies. His war experiences are told in flashback. Whenever he thinks about death, a motorcycle drives by.

A specific literary use of irony is called **dramatic irony**. In the example above, the audience knows that the soldier will die in a motorcycle crash. The soldier himself, of course, doesn't know how he will die. (A **flashback**, by the way, is another literary device made popular by the movies. Flashbacks jump back in the story's chronology to give background information. For example, the opening scene of the film *Lord of the Rings: Return of the King* shows Gollum before he found the ring.)

Foreshadowing

A soldier goes to war. He survives many brutal battles, just barely missing being killed several times. The soldier becomes obsessed with his "good luck"—why does he survive when so many others die? Every time the soldier has a brush with death, the author makes some subtle mention of a black motorcycle. Eventually, the soldier's best friend is killed in a motorcycle crash the day after the war has ended. The soldier himself comes home and not too long afterward, he dies by crashing his motorcycle.

In this example, the audience and character are equally ignorant about the outcome of the story. However, by using **foreshadowing**, the author begins to clue in his audience. The character's fate is slowly revealed to the audience but not necessarily to the character himself.

Note that the ending to this story is doubly ironic—was the soldier "meant" to die in a motorcycle crash or did he bring it about through his own guilt about surviving while others perished? The theme of free will versus predetermination underlies this little story.

Motif

The motorcycle in the last two examples.

A **motif** is a symbol that is carried through an entire work of fiction. The motorcycle symbolized death throughout both stories. In the *Lord of the Rings*, the One Ring is a motif for the corrupting nature of power.

Now that you have all these concepts under your belt, it's time to learn the most efficient way to use your knowledge on testlike items and sets.

ESSENTIAL STRATEGIES

RP sets consist of two elements: passages and items. Therefore, we must learn how to handle the passages and the items separately. We'll use a long nonfiction RP to introduce the key methods you'll want to use for tackling each element. Then we'll turn to short RPs, paired RPs, and fiction RPs to show you how to modify the methods to handle these "special cases."

Generally, you'll want to deal with the passage before you look at the items. As you read through the next sections on how to tackle the passage, keep in mind the major types of items you'll be asked to answer:

- Recognizing the major features of an RP: **topic, main idea, purpose, tone, theme, and logic**.
- Recognizing the use of rhetorical devices and literary techniques, including: **hyperbole, repetition, imagery and figurative language, sound patterns, rhetorical questions, idioms and clichés, irony, foreshadowing, and motif**.
- Decoding unfamiliar words from context.
- Finding informational details (facts) in the passage.
- Identifying cause and effect and follow the logic of arguments.
- Comparing and contrasting arguments.

SKIMMING

Before we get to our step methods for passages and items, we'd like to introduce a critical skill that is key to your success when tackling RPs: skimming.

Because of the time constraints, SAT reading is not like normal, everyday reading. Normal, everyday *reading* means reading every single word of a passage at least once. *Skimming* means reading only some of the words in a passage and letting your eyes dart across the rest.

We know you know how to read—but do you know how to skim? Many students are never taught this valuable skill. The key to skimming is breaking the habit of reading a passage word for word. This is an essential skill for succeeding on RPs, because it leads to significant time savings. It is one of several essential *strategies* you'll need to maximize your score.

Here's how you do it:

* *Read* only the first and last sentences in paragraphs.
* Circle or underline signpost words or key terms. Terms deemed as "key" will vary from reader to reader, but the idea is to identify some important terms, as well as those important signpost words.
* Use your pencil to help you break the habit of reading every word. Move the tip of your pencil across the lines of text quickly enough to make it impossible for you to read every word. This forces you to skip over some words and phrases, which means you are actually *skimming*.

TACKLING THE LONG PASSAGE

Long passages adhere to a pretty rigid structure:

* Paragraph 1: Introduction/proposition.
* Paragraph 2: First point in support of proposed argument with supporting data. Transition sentence.
* Paragraph 3: Second point in support of proposed argument with supporting data. Transition sentence.

And so forth. (There may or may not be a conclusion included in the excerpt.)

The first chunk will almost certainly contain the main idea of the whole passage; the first sentence of each subsequent paragraph usually contains at least some hint of the main idea of that paragraph; and the last sentence of each paragraph usually provides a transition to the next point. Now this won't *always* be the case, but it is the case often enough to make the reading vs. skimming time savings an excellent bet for the savvy test-taker.

Knowing which parts of a passage you need to actually read and which you can skim is a crucial part of getting the most points you can on RPs. Follow this method every time you encounter a Long RP:

Step 1: *Read* **the italicized introduction.**

Step 2: *Read* **only the first quarter of the passage. Jot down the key features of this chunk.**

Step 3: *Skim* **every subsequent paragraph. Jot down the main idea of each paragraph.**

By "key features," we mean the topic, main idea, purpose, and tone of the passage.

Let's look at the rationale for this method in more detail.

1. *Read* the italicized introduction. The italicized introduction sets the stage for the passage you're about to read. Never skip it: the introduction is your first clue to the topic, scope, and main idea.

2. *Read* only the first quarter of the passage. Jot down the key features of this chunk. The vast majority of passages give at least some idea of the topic, scope, main idea, and sometimes even the purpose in the first quarter of the passage. "Quarter" is a loose distinction— don't count up the lines and divide by four. The combination of reading the italicized introduction and the first chunk of the passage will give you most of the key information you need to answer many of the items you'll encounter.

   As you tackle a passage, you want to maintain mental focus and get the most information you can out of the passage. Jotting down key words or short phrases in the margins of your test booklet forces you to engage with the text. Jotting down notes also prevents you from losing focus and zoning out. Losing focus means rereading, which wastes valuable time, and as you know, wasting time is the cardinal sin on standardized tests. In addition to jotting down the main idea, you can also circle key words or underline them. Experiment with the practice material at the end of this book and do what works best for you.

3. *Skim* every subsequent paragraph. Jot down the key features of each paragraph. Remember, skimming means:
   • Read only the first and last sentences in paragraphs.
   • Circle or underline signpost words or key terms.

- Use your pencil to help you break the habit of reading every word.

As you skim across the surface of the text, be on the lookout for (circling/ underlining) key words and terms and for signpost words that signal a shift in the argument.

Reading Actively

Notice how our step method to tackling passages encourages mental concentration and efficiency by making reading something more than just moving your line of sight across the page. The physical act of reading in this way, which includes doing a little bit of writing (i.e., jotting), engages other parts of your brain and body. This keeps you from zoning out and increases concentration.

The goal here is for you to maintain the level of concentration you normally experience when you read in untimed situations. When you're really into a book or an article, the rest of the world fades away and you disappear into the page. Unfortunately, time constraints and the pressure of knowing you're being tested make it difficult to maintain this kind of natural, high-level concentration. Reading actively in the manner we've described builds your concentration.

Tackling the Passage in Slow Motion

We'd like you to read the following abbreviated passage. We created this passage by excluding those parts of the full passage that you shouldn't read word for word. We've used **bold** text to denote circling/underlining. In other words, we've applied the passage-tackling step method for you.

As you read, jot down the key features of the various chunks of the passage in the margin. Make sure to time yourself down to the second. Note *exactly* how long it takes you to read the passage in the space provided at the end the passage.

Abbreviated Passage: 478 Words, including Italicized Introduction

The following passage is taken from an article on the architecture of the **Etruscans, a tribe that dominated Italy before the rise of the Romans**, *and the* **Roman architect Vitruvius'** On Architecture, *which was written in the first century* B.C. *during the reign of the* **emperor Augustus.**

As we have seen, decades of archeological research have shown that Vitruvius' famous chapter on Etruscan temples **idealized readily apparent diversity.** While Vitruvius did accurately capture the main features of the **Etruscan** style, actual Etruscan temples deviated quite significantly from his ideal. We might ask **why Vitruvius ignored the architectural diversity** of the many different Etruscan temples with which he clearly was familiar. Answering this question provides some useful insight into **not only Vitruvius' definition of the Etruscan style but also the purpose of** *On Architecture* **as a whole.**

Traditionally, scholars answered this question by pointing to Vitruvius' allegiance to **Greek philosophy.** In chapter six, Vitruvius reports that he has had the benefit of a liberal Greek education, which he recommends to all aspiring architects. Without such broad training, Vitruvius argues, no architect can understand proper architectural theory. For Vitruvius, **architectural theory rested on the principles of mathematical proportion** promulgated by such Greek philosophers as Pythagoras. These philosophers believed that the universe was structured according to god-given mathematical laws. ... **macrocosm ... microcosm ... proportionality ... Thus, ... correspondences ... body ... temple.** Vitruvius Hellenized the Etruscan temple by **superimposing** Greek notions of mathematical proportionality on his purportedly empirical description of the Etruscan temple style.

Vitruvius' belief that specific natural proportions should be extended to architectural forms **does help to explain** why he idealized Etruscan temples.... **However, far more mundane considerations** acted in concert with Vitruvius' allegiance to Greek notions of mathematical harmony to encourage the idealization of the Etruscan temple.

Despite its title, *On Architecture* was **not written primarily for architects.** ... **Augustus ... patron ... busy ...: ... read the introductions ... skip the rest** ... One quickly realizes that the chapter introductions constitute **an ancient résumé** designed to **convince Augustus to entrust part of his architectural legacy to Vitruvius.**

Moreover, one must also keep in mind that *On Architecture*, like all ancient books, was originally published as a series of **scrolls.** ... **"chapter"** ... **inconvenient ... front-load ... important ideas** ... The ancient author had to earn each "unrolling" by concentrating that much more on the **order in which ideas were presented** and **the economy with which they were expressed**—and how much more so when one's **intended audience is the emperor** of Rome?

Vitruvius' idealization of Etruscan temples now becomes **even more understandable. Tellingly ... relatively unimportant ... In order to ... attention ... patronage ... digestible package ... This fact,** along with Vitruvius' fundamental belief in proportionality, **goes a long way toward explaining** why Vitruvius ignored the architectural diversity he doubtless saw in Etruscan temples.

Time:

Here's our version of the margin notes:

First "quarter": the italicized intro to the first paragraph; a chunk of the second paragraph*	Vitr. and Etruscan temples—why no diversity—why did he simplify in his book? 1st reason: traditional; Greek proportionality
Paragraph 3	another reason—more mundane
Paragraph 4	O.A. not for archs—it's V.'s résumé
Paragraph 5	O.A. originally scrolls, not book
Paragraph 6	résumé + scrolls = another reason for lack of diversity in Et. temples

* Remember to be flexible in defining the first quarter. There is no hard-and-fast rule to this designation. In this case, we started skimming as soon as we hit what looked like supporting data in the second paragraph.

In the chart above, we've tried to mimic the jotting style of margin notes. You certainly don't need to make a chart; you'll be scribbling in the margins only. Your jottings were likely even more compressed and abbreviated, and rightly so. For example, a more realistic version of our notes for the first quarter would be:

V. and Et temps—no div—why? 1. trad scholars: Gk. proportion.

Scribbling that would take about three seconds. Be as economical as you can and remember: the only person who needs to understand your notes is you.

Now, fill in the chart below as best you can, referring to your (and our, if you like) margin notes on the main idea of each chunk of the passage.

Topic	
Main Idea	

Purpose	
Tone	

Notice how you got quite a bit of key information out of this abbreviated passage.

Do you really have to write down the topic, main idea, and so forth? That's a matter of judgment. It's possible that after enough practice, you'll start noting these four major features of each passage automatically and mentally. But as you begin to practice, force yourself to write them down, if only to train yourself to look for these major features.

An Experiment

Now, read the full, unabbreviated passage word for word. Again, time yourself and note the time in the space below the passage.

Full, Unabbreviated Passage: 776 Words, including Italicized Introduction

The following passage is taken from an article on the architecture of the Etruscans, a tribe that dominated Italy before the rise of the Romans, and the Roman architect Vitruvius' On Architecture, which was written in the first century B.C. during the reign of the emperor Augustus.

As we have seen, decades of archeological research have shown that Vitruvius' famous chapter on Etruscan temples idealized readily apparent diversity. While Vitruvius did accurately capture the main features of the Etruscan style, actual Etruscan temples deviated quite significantly from his ideal. We might ask why Vitruvius ignored the
5   architectural diversity of the many different Etruscan temples with which he clearly was familiar. Answering this question provides some useful insight into not only Vitruvius' definition of the Etruscan style but also the purpose of *On Architecture* as a whole.

    Traditionally, scholars answered this question by pointing to
10   Vitruvius' allegiance to Greek philosophy. In chapter six, Vitruvius reports that he has had the benefit of a liberal Greek education, which he recommends to all aspiring architects. Without such broad training, Vitruvius argues, no architect can understand proper architectural theory. For Vitruvius, architectural theory rested on the principles of
15   mathematical proportion promulgated by such Greek

philosophers as Pythagoras. These philosophers believed that the universe was structured according to god-given mathematical laws. They further believed that the harmonious mathematical structure of the universe (the *macrocosm*) was reflected in the structure of the human body (the *microcosm*). Vitruvius extended this reflection to architectural forms. Temples, Vitruvius believed, must reflect the mathematical proportionality of the body, just as the body reflects the mathematical proportionality of the universe. Thus, Vitruvius claimed to "find" correspondences between proportional measurements of the human body—that the hand's length is one-tenth the body's height, for example—and proportional measurements of the Etruscan temple. Vitruvius Hellenized the Etruscan temple by superimposing Greek notions of mathematical proportionality on his purportedly empirical description of the Etruscan temple style.

Vitruvius' belief that specific natural proportions should be extended to architectural forms does help to explain why he idealized Etruscan temples. After all, mathematical models generally don't allow for much deviation. However, far more mundane considerations acted in concert with Vitruvius' allegiance to Greek notions of mathematical harmony to encourage the idealization of the Etruscan temple.

Despite its title, *On Architecture* was not written primarily for architects. It was written to convince the emperor Augustus, the most powerful patron in Rome, to give Vitruvius the opportunity to do large-scale architectural work. Vitruvius knew that if Augustus devoted any time at all to *On Architecture*, the emperor would most likely do what busy executives still do to this day: he would read the introductions to each of the ten chapters and skip the rest of the book. Reading *On Architecture* in this manner—each introduction in sequence—is a revelation. One quickly realizes that the chapter introductions constitute an ancient résumé designed to convince Augustus to entrust part of his architectural legacy to Vitruvius.

Moreover, one must also keep in mind that *On Architecture*, like all ancient books, was originally published as a series of scrolls. Each modern "chapter" most likely corresponds to one ancient scroll. This physical form lent even greater significance to the snappy, pertinent introductions and the concise writing that modern readers also demand. The physical act of reading a scroll made the kind of flipping back and forth that modern paginated books allow significantly more inconvenient. Scrolls strongly encouraged ancient authors to front-load the most important ideas they wanted to convey. The ancient author had to earn each "unrolling" by concentrating that much more on the order in which ideas were presented and the economy with which they were

expressed—and how much more so when one's intended audience is the
60 emperor of Rome?

Vitruvius' idealization of Etruscan temples now becomes even more understandable. Tellingly, Vitruvius buried his discussion of Etruscan temples toward the end of a chapter (i.e., scroll), which reveals that Vitruvius considered Etruscan temples to be relatively unimportant. In
65 the unlikely event that Augustus (or his appointed reader) might have actually put in the effort to reach this discussion, the last thing Vitruvius would have wanted his exalted audience to encounter is any unnecessary detail. In order to capture Augustus' attention—and patronage—Vitruvius had to demonstrate his complete command of
70 architecture in the smallest, most easily digestible package possible. The purpose of *On Architecture* was not to record architectural variety in encyclopedic detail but rather to gain architectural commissions. This fact, along with Vitruvius' fundamental belief in proportionality, goes a long way toward explaining why Vitruvius ignored the architectural
75 diversity he doubtless saw in Etruscan temples.

Time:

Add anything you'd like to your chart:

Topic	
Main Idea	
Purpose	
Tone	

Here's how we filled in the chart:

Topic	V's book on architecture/Reasons why V ignored diversity in Etruscan temples
Main Idea	Along with traditional interpretation—V. liked Greek phil.—author adds that purpose of book (to get work for V.) and scroll-nature of book explains lack of diversity.
Purpose	To introduce another "mundane" explanation for why V ignored diversity in Etruscan temples.
Tone	respectfully academic; a discussion

Now, let's interpret the results of our experiment.

- How much more did you learn when you read the full passage?
- How much more time did it take to read the full passage?
- Compare the "cost" of the extra time that was required to read the full passage to the "reward" of whatever additional information and comprehension you gained.

While you probably gathered a little more information and gained a little more comprehension, the abbreviated passage gave you a fairly good idea of the passage's topic, main idea, purpose, and tone. Furthermore, you know roughly what each chunk of the passage is about. The information you gather from skimming the passage will allow you to answer just about every possible item, as you'll see in a subsequent section.

The take-home message here is: the significant amount of time you save by skimming will be devoted to tackling the items, which will gain you points. Reading a passage word for word is an unwise, unnecessary, and very low-yield investment. Answering items correctly is what gets you points. Items require a lot of time and attention, and the simple fact is, you don't need to understand every single word in a passage in order to answer every item correctly. Remember: you are not reading for pleasure or for school. You are reading simply to score higher on the SAT.

Now that you know how to handle the basic long passage, let's discuss the "special cases."

TACKLING THE SHORT RP

Here's the good news: short RPs are no big deal. Follow this method every time you encounter a short passage:

Step 1: Read the items before you read the passage.

Step 2: Read the italicized introduction.

Step 3: Read the entire passage, word for word.

There are two ways in which tackling short RPs differs from tackling long RPs.

First, you'll read the items *before* you read the passage. Short RPs only have two items, so it will be much easier for you to remember what the items are asking. Knowing what to look for in the passage will focus your reading, which will save you time.

Second, feel free to read the entire passage word for word. For example, if an item focuses on the overall content of the short passage, go ahead and read the whole thing. Because these passages are short, you won't waste much time by reading through the entire thing.

TACKLING THE PAIRED RP

Paired RPs also require a slightly different passage-reading and set-tackling strategy. The SAT has been kind enough to organize the items in the following manner:

- Items concerned with the first passage only come first.
- These are followed by items concerned with the second passage only.
- Finally, at the end of the set you'll find a few items that compare or contrast both passages.

A fairly obvious but very powerful strategy follows from this structure:

Step 1: Read the italicized introduction.

Step 2: Read and *skim* the first passage.

Step 3: Skip immediately to the items concerned with the first passage only.

Step 4: When you've finished these, go back and read the second passage.

Step 5: Skip to the items associated with the second passage only.

Step 6: If you have time, attempt the compare-and-contrast items.

Be flexible when you follow this strategy. "The first passage" doesn't necessarily mean Passage 1. You'll choose which passage to read first. For example, you can read the first few lines of each passage and choose the one that's easier for you. Or, you can just start with the shorter passage.

Flexibility and the experience you gain from practice should also guide how you balance reading and skimming. Each paired RP passage is shorter than a long passage, but longer than a short passage. Rather than give you a hard-and-fast rule about whether to read every word or skim, we'll let your experience and judgment, as well as the subject matter and length of a particular passage, guide you. As a rule of thumb, if you find yourself getting bogged down in details and supporting examples, skim along until you find a signpost word, term, or some indication of a new thought.

Following this method has two major benefits. First, it splits paired RPs into two scaled-down long passages. By treating each one separately, you avoid the usual danger of paired RPs, which is confusing the two passages. Remember, each passage discusses the same topic from a different perspective, so you might easily mix up the two.

As a result, you'll find yourself constantly turning back to the two passages, which is a waste of precious time. Who needs that extra pressure? The SAT is tough enough as it is.

Second, by saving the compare-and-contrast items for last, you ensure that you get all the points you can on the easier passage-specific items. As you would expect, compare-and-contrast items are tougher than passage-specific items.

TACKLING THE FICTION PASSAGE

Fiction passages will only appear as long RPs. The only major difference between fiction and nonfiction passages is that fiction is not structured as hierarchically as nonfiction. By "hierarchical," we mean the rigid structure of passages we described at the beginning of this section:

- Paragraph 1: Introduction/Proposition
- Paragraph 2: First point in support of proposed argument with supporting data. Transition sentence.
- Paragraph 3: Second point in support of proposed argument with supporting data. Transition sentence.

And so forth.

Even though you can't rely on the hierarchical structure you find in most nonfiction passages, fiction passages do contain an analogous "skeleton" that you can use to guide your reading. The key thing to keep in mind is: **"Who is doing what to whom and how does it make everyone, including the narrator, feel?"** This question focuses your attention on the key elements of conventional prose fiction. Let's review these briefly:

- **The narrator.** Think of the narrator as the "voice" that's telling the story. The SAT uses first- or third-person narration (first person: "Call me Ishmael…"; third person: "He sat on the bench bemoaning his lost love…"). It doesn't get cutesy or experimental with second-person narration ("You go to the store. You see a black cat. You freak out.") or with unreliable narrators who "lie" to the reader about what's actually happening in the story.

- **The characters.** Again, no one's going to get cutesy on you. You won't find characters disappearing into the ether because you find out in the last line that they were figments of the imagination of an unreliable narrator who turns out to be an escaped mental patient. Just keep in mind who's who, and what their relationships are (mother/daughter, friends, husband/wife, etc.).

- **The plot.** Not much can actually transpire in a passage of 800 to 850 words. If fiction scares you, let this fact calm your fears. Events will be apparent. The most you'll be asked to do is read between the lines of what characters say to one another, which is a skill you already use every day. ("Jane said I look good today. Does she really mean this, or was it a sarcastic dig?")

- **The way the author uses language to convey states of mind and events.** The section on literary techniques and rhetorical devices (pages 29–33) is more than enough preparation to handle what the SAT will throw at you.

There are two basic steps to approaching a fiction passage:

Step 1: Read the italicized introduction.

Step 2: Read the entire passage, word for word.

One advantage of SAT fiction passages is that they are usually interesting and easy to read. They're mostly about human relationships, so they don't introduce unfamiliar information or jargon, as nonfiction passages usually do. In general, go ahead and read these word for word, but read them quickly, and *always be prepared to skim when you're pressed for time*. If what you're reading seems like unnecessary information, skim ahead and pick up the story again. As you can see, you'll need to let your own strengths and experience guide you on test day. If, on the one hand, you're a fast reader who feels comfortable with fiction, go ahead and read the passage quickly (with little or no skimming) and tackle the items. If, on the other hand, you're a slow reader who's not comfortable with fiction, first do all the other items in the section and then come back to the fiction passage and try to get what you can out of a quick read/skim.

As you read, circle names of characters, key dialogue, crucial images—anything that keeps you physically and mentally engaged. Aim to get an idea of what happens where in the passage so that when you hit the items you'll have some idea of where you might need to go in the passage to puzzle out a particular item.

Above all—don't sweat it! Fiction is no big deal. Practice will help you.

TACKLING THE ITEMS

The College Board breaks RP items into three categories:

- Vocabulary-in-Context
- Literal Comprehension
- Extended Reasoning

The first two categories are quite discrete. Vocabulary-in-Context (VIC) items ask you to define a particular word based on the context in which it was used in the passage. Literal Comprehension (LC) items essentially require you to find particular data in the passage—a bit like a mini-"research" project. The idea is to test how well (and quickly) you absorb information.

The third category is the kicker. Extended Reasoning includes a huge range of potential items, the major ones being:

- Recognizing the main idea, purpose, tone, theme, topic, and logic of a passage.
- Recognizing the use of rhetorical devices and literary techniques.
- Making inferences based on the passage.
- Identifying cause and effect and following the logic of arguments.
- Comparing and contrasting arguments.

And those are just the *major* ones. Extended Reasoning encompasses pretty much anything that's not a VIC or a LC item.

We feel that the only reason to break The College Board's Extended Reasoning category into smaller subcategories is to encourage and enable the kind of pacing strategies you'll need to maximize your score. If you can identify a limited number of distinct item-stems, you'll be able to quickly scan all the item-stems in an RP and decide the order in which you'll attempt the items. We'll discuss this set-level strategy—called **Bombing Runs**—in detail in the next section.

With this strategic goal in mind, we've broken Extended Reasoning into three smaller, but still broad, categories. Those three added to VIC and LC make five item types in total:

- VIC
- LC
- Tone
- Purpose/Main Idea

- Inference

Keep in mind that there are countless other item subtypes that you'll run into throughout this book and in the practice sets. You'll be perfectly prepared to handle them as they come up if you do the following three things:

- Follow the step methods for tackling **passages** we presented in the preceding section.
- Follow the step method for tackling **items** we'll present in the following section, including Bombing Runs.
- Practice, practice, practice in order to build up your familiarity with the variety of items you might see.

Bombing Runs

Unlike some other item types on the SAT, RP items are not presented in order of difficulty. However, items that refer to words or lines in a passage are presented in the order in which those words or lines appear in the passage. For example, an item that asks about line 13 will always come before an item that asks about line 23. Items that ask about the passage as a whole, such as Main Idea/Purpose, may appear anywhere in the set.

The cardinal rule of SAT test-taking is to skip around, doing those items that are easiest first and saving the rest for last. Do **not** simply begin with the first item and work through the set in order. Never forget that every item is worth the same amount of points. So, it makes no sense to struggle with item 1 for five minutes when you could have answered items 2 through 4 correctly in the same amount of time.

The way to avoid this classic error is to fly "Bombing Runs." To illustrate this method, assume your set has ten items. Begin by reading the first item. Do not read the answers: read the **stem** only. If it seems easy, complete that item and move on to the next stem. If you encounter a challenging stem, skip that item. (Make sure to circle the entire item in your test booklet if you skip it. Also, enter answers in five-item blocks, omitting whichever you've skipped. You don't want to misgrid your answers.) After you've handled all the items that are easy for you, return to those items that you think you could figure out, given a little more time. Make another Bombing Run, skipping all of the really tough ones. Repeat your Bombing Runs until time runs out.

Tackling the Long RP Set

Make sure you attack your long RP **sets** in the following manner (we'll discuss the "special cases" later):

Step 1: Tackle the passage.

Step 2: Read *all* the item stems in the set.

Step 3: Decide which items will need the least investment and tackle those first. Leave others for last.

Tackling Individual Items

The key with all SAT items is to have some idea of the answer before you look at the answer choices. The distractors are there to do just that—distract you. Don't let that happen. Use the following method every time you attempt an RP item:

Step 1: Cover up the answer choices.

Step 2: Read the stem carefully.

Step 3: If directed to the passage, go back and read the referenced lines.

Step 4: Generate a potential answer *without* looking at the answer choices.

Step 5: Compare your potential fix or answer to the answer choices and eliminate all that do not match.

Step 6: Take a moment to double-check your selection.

Let's apply our set step method and item step method in "slow motion" to see how this all works.

Tackling the RP Set in Slow Motion

Let's work through a typical long RP set.

Step 1: Tackle the Passage.

We'll use the Vitruvius passage, which you've already tackled using our step method. Make sure to refer back to your margin notes and the charts you filled in as you work through this exercise. We'll reproduce our versions of the charts below for convenience.

First "quarter"	Vitr. and Etruscan temples—why no diversity—why did he simplify in his book? 1st reason: traditional; Greek proportionality
Paragraph 3	another reason—more mundane
Paragraph 4	O.A. not for archs—it's V.'s résumé
Paragraph 5	O.A. originally scrolls, not book
Paragraph 6	résumé + scrolls = another reason for lack of diversity in Et. Temples

Topic	V.'s book on architecture/Reasons why V. ignored diversity in Etruscan temples
Main Idea	Along with traditional interpretation—V. liked Greek phil.—author adds that purpose of book (to get work for V.) and scroll-nature of book explain lack of diversity.
Purpose	To introduce another "mundane" explanation for why V. ignored diversity in Etruscan temples.
Tone	respectfully academic; a discussion

Step 2: Read *all* the item stems in the set.

Here are the stems:

1. As used in line 12, the word "liberal" most nearly means

2. On the whole, the author's attitude toward the traditional scholarly explanation of Vitruvius' description of the Etruscan temple style described in lines 10–30 is one of

3. The principal function of the fifth paragraph (lines 48–60) is to show

4. The author would most likely agree that the physical form of ancient books

5. The main purpose of the passage is to

Step 3: Decide which items will need the least investment and tackle those first. Leave others for last.

We don't want you to spend any time categorizing the exact order in which you'll tackle all the items in the set. Doing it one by one is fine: pick the easiest item, complete it, pick the easiest item from those that remain, complete that one, and so on until you're done or time runs out. Keep in mind that it won't take you very long to read the stems, and the time you'll save and points you'll gain tackling questions according to *your* order of difficulty will more than compensate for the minute or so you'll invest.

Having said that, in order to give you an idea of the thought processes involved in this step, we'll categorize all five items at once in the following chart. This categorization is just one way of approaching the five items. When you work through practice sets, you should follow your own order based on your strengths and experience. What we want you to absorb is the importance and efficiency of doing easy items first. In general, however, you'll find that the VIC and Main Idea/Purpose items tend to require less of an investment than LC or Inference items.

Order	Item	Reason
1st	1	I'll do the VIC first. They require the least investment.
2nd	5	I already have a good idea of what the main idea and purpose of the passage are. This requires no further effort to answer.
3rd	2	I know that the traditional scholarly interpretation of Vitruvius' treatment of Etruscan temples was covered in the first chunk. I have a good idea about what this was, and I also have a sense of the passage's overall tone. A relatively low investment will likely be needed to get a point.
4th	3	Here's a Detail question that will require a little research, but which still should be a straightforward "mini-research project."
5th	4	Here's an inference question, and it requires me to take on the role of the author. This is a little tricky—but doable. I'll save it for last to ensure that I lock down the lower-investment items first.

Remember, we categorized all the items at once for instructional purposes only. You'll decide one-by-one which item to tackle as you move through the set.

Now you're ready to deal with each item.

Tackling the Items in Slow Motion

Let's apply the item step method to the items that follow. First we'll attempt each of the five items we categorized in the order we arrived at above: **1, 5, 2, 3, 4**. We'll work through these five together, noting some typical features of each. Then, we'll provide you with some more items based on the Vitruvius passage for you to work through on your own. We've provided one representative item from each of the five major item types.

Item 1, *Vocabulary-in-Context (VIC)*

Step 1: Cover up the answer choices.

1. As used in line 12, the word "liberal" most nearly means

We've done this for you. Use your hand or an index card to hide the naughty distractors from you.

Step 2: Read the stem carefully.

Pretty much all VICs look like this item.

Step 3: If directed to the passage, go back and read the referenced lines.

The key to VICs is going back to the sentence that's referenced, and often to either the sentence before, the sentence after, or both. Here it is:

> *In chapter six, Vitruvius reports that he has had the benefit of a liberal Greek education, which he recommends to all aspiring architects. Without such broad training, Vitruvius argues, no architect can understand proper architectural theory.*

What was the main idea of this chunk, anyway? That traditional scholars attributed Vitruvius' treatment of Etruscan temples to his adherence to Greek philosophical ideas of proportionality.

If you took out *liberal*, what else would work?

In chapter six, Vitruvius reports that he has had the benefit of a ___ Greek education, which he recommends to all aspiring architects. Without such broad training, Vitruvius argues, no architect can understand proper architectural theory.

Notice that the phrase *without such broad training* gives you a clue as to what the "missing" word should be.

Step 4: Generate a potential answer *without* looking at the answer choices.

You want something like "broad." Note that *liberal* is one of those words that has several common meanings. Naturally, these are the kinds of words that usually show up in VICs. This item type tests not just vocabulary, but vocabulary *in context*.

Don't fret too much about coming up with the perfect prediction. A phrase will do just fine, especially since the correct answer is often a phrase, rather than a specific word.

Step 5: Compare your potential fix or answer to the answer choices and eliminate all that do not match.

Here are the answer choices:

1.   As used in line 12, the word "liberal" most nearly means

(A)   tolerant
(B)   generous
(C)   free-thinking
(D)   wide-ranging
(E)   narrow

Most of the choices are legitimate definitions of *liberal*. But you're looking for the correct definition **in context**. That's exactly why you want to arm yourself with a prediction before you even look at the choices.

E is exactly the opposite of what you're looking for. Eliminate it. (You'll very often see the opposite of what you're looking for in the answer choices.) **A**, **B**, and **C** also do not match your prediction, "broad." **D** works.

Step 6: Take a moment to double-check your selection.

Plug *wide-ranging* back into the sentence as a check. (You'll do this in your head, of course.)

> In chapter six, Vitruvius reports that he has had the benefit of a *wide-ranging* Greek education, which he recommends to all aspiring architects. Without such broad training, Vitruvius argues, no architect can understand proper architectural theory.

Don't skip this step! It takes a second and can save you 1 point (If you catch an error in your thinking at this stage, you'll gain a point where you might have lost a quarter-point for a 1-point turnaround). That's a pretty good time investment.

Item 5, *Main Idea/Purpose*

Step 1: Cover up the answer choices.

> 5.   The main purpose of the passage is to

Step 2: Read the stem carefully.

Main Idea/Purpose items vary a little in form, but they're easily identifiable. Phrases like "main idea," "primary purpose," and "main point" identify this item type.

Step 3: If directed to the passage, go back and read the referenced lines.

Not applicable here. This is a "global" item that asks about the passage as a whole. Most long RP sets contain a Main Idea/Purpose item.

Step 4: Generate a potential answer *without* looking at the answer choices.

What did we determine the purpose to be?

> *To introduce another "mundane" explanation for why Vitruvius ignored diversity in Etruscan temples.*

By tackling the passage in the manner we suggested, you already have a ready-made potential answer with no extra effort!

Step 5: Compare your potential fix or answer to the answer choices and eliminate all that do not match.

Here are the answer choices:

5. The main purpose of the passage is to

(A)   expose Vitruvius' dishonesty
(B)   prove the value of a Greek education
(C)   suggest that Vitruvius considered Etruscan temples to be the most important type of temple
(D)   discuss the differences between ancient scrolls and modern books
(E)   account for the difference between Vitruvius' written description of Etruscan temples and their archaeological remains

Before we settle on an answer choice, we want you to notice a couple of things. First, notice how the first word in each answer choice is a verb:

(A)   **expose** Vitruvius' dishonesty
(B)   **prove** the value of a Greek education
(C)   **suggest** that Vitruvius considered Etruscan temples to be the most important type of temple
(D)   **discuss** the differences between ancient scrolls and modern books
(E)   **account** for the difference between Vitruvius' written description of Etruscan temples and their archaeological remains

Which verb matches the author's purpose most closely? You can eliminate **A** right off the bat. It doesn't match the passage's tone. (As we noted earlier, tone and purpose bleed into and play off of each other.) Answer choices with extreme language tend to be incorrect (we'll return to this point later on).

Choice **B** is a distortion. Since so many distractors boil down to distortions of the text, it's worth teasing out exactly how this nasty little distractor does its dastardly distorting duty.

One typical distortion technique is to purposely mix up beliefs that the author holds with beliefs held by the people the author discusses. In the passage, the author mentions that *Vitruvius* valued a Greek education. The author's opinion is neither stated nor relevant. The reason the author mentions a Greek education is to present the traditional scholarly interpretation of Vitruvius' treatment of Etruscan temples. If you were pressed for time you might have grabbed for **B** simply because it "looks familiar." That's how RP item distractors seduce you, so be warned!

Choice **C** is another typical distractor. It states the exact opposite of what the passage states. The author noted that the fact that Vitruvius buried his discussion of Etruscan temples at the end of a book (i.e., scroll) most likely means that Vitruvius didn't think it very important.

(By the way, whether or not you agree with that judgment isn't important—what matters is what the author thinks. This is true of all RPs. Not only must you keep the author's beliefs separate from the beliefs of the people he discusses, but you must also keep your *own* opinions out of it as well. You're being tested on how much you can gather from the text, not what you know about the topic.)

Choice **D** is yet another typical distractor. It's perfectly true that the author discusses the differences between ancient scrolls and modern books. But is that the *main purpose* of the passage? What is supporting what here? This distractor tries to pass a supporting notion off as the main purpose of the passage. The SAT wants to make sure you understand the hierarchical nature of written arguments. It's a key feature of effective nonfiction prose writing.

Well, there's not much suspense left now, is there? Choice **E** matches your prediction very nicely. That statement encompasses the entire passage. It includes both the discussion of the traditional explanation and the author's own complementary explanation.

But notice one thing choices **B**, **C**, and **D** have in common. Each of them puts forward a subordinate or secondary feature of the passage as the *main*, overarching purpose or point. Since you know that this is a Main Idea/Purpose item, a subordinate feature of the passage can't be right.

Step 6: Take a moment to double-check your selection.

Silently reading the stem-plus-answer choice as a full sentence is good enough:

> The main purpose of the passage is to account for the difference between Vitruvius' written description of Etruscan temples and their archaeological remains.

Sounds good!

Item 2, *Tone*

Step 1: Cover up the answer choices.

2. On the whole, the author's attitude toward the traditional scholarly explanation of Vitruvius' description of the Etruscan temple style described in lines 10–30 is one of

Step 2: Read the stem carefully.

Tone items focus on the author. How does the author feel about his subject or the people or ideas he's discussing?

Step 3: If directed to the passage, go back and read the referenced lines.

By reading the first line in the third paragraph when you tackled the passage, you learned that the author felt that the traditional explanation is a pretty good one:

Vitruvius' belief that specific natural proportions should be extended to architectural forms helps to explain why he idealized Etruscan temples.

Step 4: Generate a potential answer *without* looking at the answer choices.

What's the author's general tone? When we tackled the passage, we wrote:

respectfully academic; a discussion

That certainly holds in this specific instance as well. Once again, the information you gathered by reading and skimming the passage provides a good prediction to one of the items with no extra effort required.

Step 5: Compare your potential fix or answer to the answer choices and eliminate all that do not match.

Here are the answer choices:

> 2. On the whole, the author's attitude toward the traditional scholarly explanation of Vitruvius' description of the Etruscan temple style described in lines 10–30 is one of
>
> (A) indifference
> (B) respect
> (C) frustration
> (D) interest
> (E) mistrust

In this case, **B** jumps right out.

Let's say you hadn't nailed down the tone as precisely as we did. Let's say all you knew was that it was "good" rather than "bad." That's very useful information! You can eliminate any choice that contains a negative word: **A**, **C**, and **E**. Now you have a 50-50 shot at getting a point. Furthermore, you might notice that *interest* is not quite specific enough. One could show interest and still take on quite a negative tone.

Step 6: Take a moment to double-check your selection.

In this case, this step is lightning-quick. You know you've got the right answer; simply pause for a split second to make sure.

Item 3, *LC*

Step 1: Cover up the answer choices.

> 3. The principal function of the fifth paragraph (lines 48–60) is to show

Step 2: Read the stem carefully.

We've described LC items as mini-research projects. You're told where to go in the passage. The combination of your margin notes and a little research will give you the answer.

Step 3: If directed to the passage, go back and read the referenced lines.

In this case, you're asked why a particular paragraph is included in the passage. As with almost all RP items, knowing the main idea of the passage sets the stage for success. Our margin note for paragraph five was:

O.A. originally scrolls, not book

The scroll-vs.-book point is brought up in support of the author's "mundane" explanation for Vitruvius' treatment of Etruscan temples. (The other point was the résumé-like nature of *On Architecture* as a whole.)

Since this is a paragraph-level detail item, you don't need to actually go back and read the referenced lines, another benefit of tackling the passage as we suggest.

Step 4: Generate a potential answer *without* looking at the answer choices.

The scroll-vs.-book point is brought up in support of the author's "mundane" explanation for Vitruvius' treatment of Etruscan temples. Specifically, the physical act of reading scrolls shaped how ancient authors organized their writings.

Step 5: Compare your potential fix or answer to the answer choices and eliminate all that do not match.

Here are the answer choices:

3. The principal function of the fifth paragraph (lines 48–60) is to show

(A) that contemporary architects did not find *On Architecture* helpful to their work

(B) why Vitruvius ended up building so many structures for Augustus

(C) how Vitruvius constructed *On Architecture*'s ten chapters with his audience's likely reading habits in mind

(D) that Augustus was as busy as any modern-day executive

(E) how the nature of ancient scrolls discouraged readers

Choice **A** is one of those nasty distortions. We don't know that contemporary architects didn't find Vitruvius' book helpful. All the author said was that architects weren't Vitruvius' primary audience. Furthermore, even if he *had* said that, it's beside the point: this paragraph is about scrolls, not intended audience. Choice **B** is also a distortion: we don't know whether Vitruvius did or did not end up getting architectural commissions. All we know is that the author maintains that this was what Vitruvius was trying to do.

Choice **C** looks pretty good. Keep it in mind, but take the time to look at all the answer choices. That keeps you from being tricked by a particularly seductive distractor; it's worth the extra few seconds.

Choice **D** is tricky because it's a perfectly legitimate inference. But this paragraph is not primarily concerned with Augustus. Rather, it's concerned with Vitruvius. It's about why Vitruvius constructed his treatise in the way that he did. He did so because he knew that his likely audience would be very busy, but the fact that his audience would be very busy is not the point. It's a small distinction but a real one. The nastiest distractors make distinctions such as these. By keeping the main idea of the entire passage in mind, you'll be able to distinguish between the correct answer and very seductive distractors like this one. The worst thing that could happen is you guess between two answer choices, which is not a bad situation to be in.

Choice **E** is an easier distractor to spot. We don't know that scrolls *discouraged readers*. This is an unwarranted inference from the statement that the physical nature of scrolls *encouraged* ancient *authors* to construct their books in a particular fashion.

Step 6: Take a moment to double-check your selection.

Combine the stem with choice **C** by reading the full sentence to yourself:

> The principal function of the fifth paragraph is to show how Vitruvius constructed *On Architecture*'s ten chapters with his audience's likely reading habits in mind.

Sounds good!

Item 4, *Inference*

Step 1: Cover up the answer choices.

4. The author would most likely agree that the physical form of ancient books

Step 2: Read the stem carefully.

Inferences require a bit of thought. Since this is a key reading skill, you'll find a few of them in each RP set. This particular example requires you to "role-play." In order to answer this item correctly, you need to get inside the head of the author and decide what he or she would "most likely" think, based on what you know from the passage. Again, the author's main idea and purpose lie behind this particular item. These items require creative and flexible thinking.

This example includes typical phrases you'll find in Inference items. These phrases include:

- "The author would most likely . . . "
- "The author implies . . . "
- "The passage implies . . . "
- "The implication of . . . "
- "It can be inferred from the passage that . . . "
- "The author suggests . . . "

This isn't a complete list, of course, but you get the idea.

Step 3: If directed to the passage, go back and read the referenced lines.

Many inference items are "global" and don't include references. As you'll see in the next step, though, that doesn't mean you shouldn't go back to the passage.

Step 4: Generate a potential answer _without_ looking at the answer choices.

When you're dealing with Inference items, this step needs to be understood a little more loosely. It's difficult to precisely predict what the answer will be. There are many possible ways to complete this stem accurately. This is usually what freaks people out, causing them to skip these items altogether or to immediately dive into the dangerous waters of the answer choices, where nasty distractors are on the lookout for panicky test-takers.

However, these possibilities are limited by the specific function that the scroll-form of ancient books plays in this passage. So, for this step, simply step back and remind yourself of what this function was. In our margin notes we wrote: "O.A. originally scrolls, not book." In order to flesh this out a bit so that we're not thrown by distractors, now would be a good time to go back to where scrolls are discussed and read (word-for-word this time) the parts we originally skimmed. We'll reproduce that paragraph here:

> Moreover, one must also keep in mind that *On Architecture*, like all ancient books, was originally published as a series of scrolls. Each modern "chapter" most likely corresponds to one ancient scroll. This physical form lent even greater significance to the snappy, pertinent introductions and the concise writing that modern readers also demand. The physical act of reading a scroll made the kind of flipping back and forth that modern paginated books allow significantly more inconvenient. Scrolls strongly encouraged ancient authors to front-load the most important ideas they wanted to convey. The ancient author had to earn each "unrolling" by concentrating that much more on the order in which ideas were presented and the economy with which they were expressed—and how much more so when one's intended audience is the emperor of Rome?

OK. The main point here is that scrolls made ancient writers more mindful of the organization and presentation of their ideas than modern writers since reading a scroll was a bit more inconvenient than reading a modern book. So our answer choice should somehow reflect this point.

Before we go on, notice that this item requires a bit of reading and thought. And we haven't even hit the answer choices yet. This is exactly why Bombing Runs are so important. Never, ever forget that each item is worth the same amount. This fact leads to a key *inference*: you should *always* answer all the items that require the least investment first.

Step 5: Compare your potential fix or answer to the answer choices and eliminate all that do not match.

Here are the answer choices:

4. The author would most likely agree that the physical form of ancient books

    (A)   prevented ancient authors from writing as well as modern authors

    (B)   encouraged the writing of encyclopedic overviews

    (C)   was responsible for the spread of ancient knowledge

    (D)   is a unique source of insight into ancient writing largely ignored by traditional scholars

    (E)   undermined the ability of ancient authors to gain patrons

Choice **A** is an unwarranted inference. For all we know from this passage, the author might even think that ancient authors were superior to their modern counterparts since scrolls required ancient authors to pay a lot of attention to how they structured their writings. But we simply don't know what the author thought because he gives no hint of a preference between ancient and modern writers.

Choice **B** is the exact opposite of what the passage states. Scrolls forced ancient writers to put the most important information at the beginning of their "chapters" and discouraged including unnecessary detail. Notice that the mention of "encyclopedic detail" occurs in the last paragraph. You may or may not have noted this when you tackled the passage. But if you didn't catch that mention, your knowledge of the main idea of the passage and of this paragraph gives you the information you need to eliminate this choice.

Choice **C** is what we refer to as a "left-field" choice. You can usually count on at least one choice being so way out in left field that it's relatively easy to eliminate. Being "out in left field" is another way of saying, "outside the scope of the passage." Here's one specific instance in which "scope" comes into play. Once you eliminate even one choice as being wrong, even if you can't go any further, you should guess from the remaining four. You'll be ahead of the wrong-answer penalty. Every little piece of test-taking strategy helps. As you practice, you'll get better and better at knowing instinctively when to pull which "tool" out of your "toolbox." In fact, that's the main benefit of practice, as we'll discuss in a later section.

Choice **D** looks pretty good. The author presents the scroll-nature of ancient books as a novel source of insight into the content and structure of ancient writing, and specifically Vitruvius' *On Architecture*. While the author accepts the validity of the traditional scholarly interpretation, which is based on Vitruvius' adherence to Greek philosophy, the author's purpose is to present a new, different, but complementary explanation based on more "mundane" considerations.

Choice **E** is a typical distortion. You've heard the proverb "Don't compare apples and oranges." Well, distractors like these do something quite similar: "apples" and "oranges" are combined. Sure, the passage argues that the desire to gain Augustus as a patron drove Vitruvius' writing (the "apple"). But this point is completely separate from the nature of writing for scrolls, as opposed to modern books (the "orange"). Distractors like these merely associate terms and concepts from the passage in order to lure you into making a mistake.

Step 6: Take a moment to double-check your selection.

Combine the stem with choice **D** by reading the full sentence to yourself:

> The author would most likely agree that the physical form of ancient books is a unique source of insight into ancient writing largely ignored by traditional scholars.

Excellent!

Now that you've gotten a taste of each of the five main item types and of the item-specific step method, let's briefly discuss some helpful "backward strategies." Then, we'll let you loose on some more items so you can begin to practice what you've learned.

Backward Strategies for RP Items

As you've already gathered, RPs are quite complex. The passages require special attention, and the items feature a lot of variety and demand quite a bit of thought and flexibility. It's impossible to anticipate every potential scenario you might find yourself in. Thankfully, it's also unnecessary. Along with the essential concepts and strategies we've just presented, we also have some powerful backward strategies.

Backward strategies are strategies you can apply when you're either having trouble applying the standard step method or when you're running out of time. It's best to present these strategies, some of which we've already alluded to, as "tools" for your "toolbox," which you can pull out if and when you need them. Add these important tips to your list of essential concepts and strategies, and you will be in an excellent position to maximize your score.

Always keep the main idea and primary purpose of the passage uppermost in your mind. Even for those items that are not explicitly "global," knowing the main idea/purpose can help you eliminate distractors in a pinch. Keeping the main idea/purpose in mind can also help you when you're having trouble formulating a potential correct answer too. So, when in doubt, step back and consider the main idea and purpose.

After all, the SAT is concerned with how well and how quickly you can figure out what's going on in a passage you've never seen before. The test-makers (as well as colleges and universities) know that given enough time you can get all the detailed information you need out of any written material. That's not really what they're interested in.

A related tip is to consider the *scope* of the topic presented. Distractors that are "out in left field"—i.e., outside the scope—are almost always wrong and can be safely eliminated in order to narrow the field of choices for an educated guess.

Choices with "extreme" language are usually wrong. Look   at the following chart:

Time	Space or Amount
Never	None
Rarely	A little/few
Sometimes	Some
Often/frequently	A lot/most
Always	All

The extreme terms are at the top and bottom of this chart; the middle terms are more measured, and therefore more likely to be correct when applied to any statement.

Another key term is *only*. This doesn't quite fit into the chart above but realize that it has a very restrictive meaning, and is "extreme" in the sense we're discussing now. For example, if I say, "The Beatles were the only worthwhile rock group that was active in the 1960s," well, that's a pretty extreme statement. All you would need to do to refute that statement is present a halfway-decent argument that any other 1960s rock group was "worthwhile."

Since we're discussing words you might find in a stem, we might as well mention *EXCEPT* and *NOT*. The SAT always capitalizes these words when they're in a stem. The test-makers do not want to trick you, but sometimes they do want to throw in a twist to test your ability to reverse the logic in a passage. You may want to leave EXCEPT/NOT items for last, but keep an eye out for them in any event.

For VICs, when in doubt, eliminate the choice that contains the most common meaning of the word in question. Consider why this should be the case. VICs are not a direct test of vocabulary knowledge. VICs use vocabulary to test your comprehension of the context in which vocabulary is used. They cannot be answered without referring to the passage. So, VIC choices must contain at least two legitimate definitions of the word in question, or else test-takers could simply select the one legitimate definition without referring to the passage at all. Finally, if the most common definition of the word in question were always the correct choice, VICs would not do a very good job of using vocabulary to test your comprehension of the context in which the word appears. The correct choices tend to be less common definitions of the word in question. Therefore, if you're stumped, eliminate the choice that contains the most common meaning—the meaning that would be listed first in the dictionary, so to speak—and go with one of the other choices.

OK. Your "toolbox" is almost full. It's time to unleash you on a few items you haven't seen so you can start practicing what you've learned.

Guided and Independent Practice

We provide three more items below based on the Vitruvius passage. We've selected the order in which you'll attempt them. You'll have ample opportunity to fly Bombing Runs on the passage sets in the back of the book. We guide you through the first two items. You'll attempt the third on your own.

Each item is preceded by the relevant excerpt from the passage. We present these excerpts only to make clear what each stem refers to. **You don't need to read the entire excerpt.** Once you've read and understood each stem below, go to the next section, "Guided Practice: Item 6," and begin.

24   . . . . Thus, Vitruvius claimed to "find" correspondences between proportional measurements of the human body—that the hand's length is one-tenth the body's height, for

27   example—and proportional measurements of the Etruscan temple.

6. In lines 24–27, the author most likely uses quotation marks in order to

(A) imply that Vitruvius purposely invented correspondences between proportional measurements of the human body and proportional measurements of the Etruscan temple that he knew didn't exist

(B) underscore the unimportance of Greek philosophy in Vitruvius' treatise

(C) suggest that Vitruvius' background in Greek philosophy prepared him to notice the types of proportional correspondences between the human body and the Etruscan temple he writes about

(D) show that Vitruvius didn't mention proportional correspondences between the human body and the Etruscan temple in his treatise

(E) emphasize Vitruvius' fundamental mistake in his discussion of Etruscan temples

Despite its title, *On Architecture* was not written primarily for architects. It was written to convince the emperor Augustus, the most powerful patron in Rome, to give Vitruvius the opportunity to do large-scale architectural work. Vitruvius knew that if Augustus devoted any time at all to *On Architecture*, the emperor would most likely do what busy executives still do to this day: he would read the introductions to each of the ten chapters and skip the rest of the book. Reading *On Architecture* in this manner—each introduction in sequence—is a revelation. One quickly realizes that the chapter introductions constitute an ancient résumé designed to convince Augustus to entrust part of his architectural legacy to Vitruvius.

7. Which of the following, if true, would most clearly strengthen the author's assertion that the introductions to *On Architecture* constitute an ancient résumé (lines 37–47)?

(A) The chapter introductions in *On Architecture* mostly discuss technical matters of architecture.

(B) The chapter introductions of other ancient treatises on architecture tend to advertise their author's qualifications, knowledge, and experience.

(C) The chapter introductions in *On Architecture* consist of a critique of buildings commissioned by Augustus which have already been completed.

(D) The latter portion of each chapter in *On Architecture* contains extended discussion of Vitruvius' various accomplishments and wide-ranging knowledge of architecture.

(E) The chapter introductions in *On Architecture* feature discussions of Vitruvius' qualifications, knowledge, and experience.

31   Vitruvius' belief that specific natural proportions should be extended to architectural forms does help to explain why he idealized Etruscan temples. After all, mathematical models generally don't allow for much deviation. However, far more mundane considerations acted in concert
35 with Vitruvius' allegiance to Greek notions of mathematical harmony to
36 encourage the idealization of the Etruscan temple.

8. Which of the following most accurately describes the organization of the third paragraph (lines 31–36)?

(A) One explanation of a situation is refuted and another is suggested.

(B) An alternative explanation is supported by evidence.

(C) An explanation of a situation is determined to be helpful but incomplete.

(D) An explanation of a situation is used to predict future events.

(E) Two opposing explanations are reconciled with each other.

Guided Practice: Item 6

Try this one on your own.

Step 1: Cover up the answer choices.

Here is the stem by itself:

6. In line 24–27, the author most likely uses quotation marks in order to

Step 2: Read the stem carefully.

What kind of item is this? Circle one of the following, or, alternatively, cross out those options that you know this item doesn't represent.

VIC

LC

Tone

Purpose/Main Idea

Inference

Step 3: If directed to the passage, go back and read the referenced lines.

Here's the paragraph that contains the referenced lines:

Traditionally, scholars answered this question by pointing to Vitruvius' allegiance to Greek philosophy. In chapter six, Vitruvius reports that he has had the benefit of a liberal Greek education, which he recommends to all aspiring architects. Without such broad training, Vitruvius argues, no architect can understand proper architectural theory. For Vitruvius, architectural theory rested on the principles of mathematical proportion promulgated by such Greek philosophers as Pythagoras. These philosophers believed that the universe was structured according to god-given mathematical laws. They further believed that the harmonious mathematical structure of the universe (the macrocosm) was reflected in the structure of the human body (the microcosm). Vitruvius extended this reflection to architectural forms. Temples, Vitruvius believed, must reflect the mathematical proportionality of the body, just as the body reflects the mathematical proportionality of the universe. **Thus, Vitruvius claimed to "find" correspondences between proportional measurements of the human body—that the hand's length is one-tenth the body's height, for example—and proportional measurements of the Etruscan temple.** Vitruvius Hellenized the Etruscan temple by superimposing Greek notions of mathematical proportionality on his purportedly empirical description of the Etruscan temple style.

You may refer back to your margin notes as well. Also, here are our margin notes and notes on main idea, tone, etc.:

First "quarter"	Vitr. And Etruscan temples—why no diversity—why did he simplify in his book? 1st reason: traditional; Greek proportionality
Paragraph 3	Another reason—more mundane
Paragraph 4	O.A. not for archs—it's V.'s résumé
Paragraph 5	O.A. originally scrolls, not book
Paragraph 6	résumé + scrolls = another reason for lack of diversity in Et. Temples

Topic	V's book on architecture/Reasons why V. ignored diversity in Etruscan temples
Main Idea	Along with traditional interpretation—V. liked Greek phil.—author adds that purpose of book (to get work for V.) and scroll-nature of book explain lack of diversity.
Purpose	To introduce another "mundane" explanation for why V. ignored diversity in Etruscan temples.
Tone	respectfully academic; a discussion

Step 4: Generate a potential answer *without* looking at the answer choices.

Jot down some notes that quickly explain why the author used quotes around the word *find* in the space provided below:

Step 5: Compare your potential fix or answer to the answer choices and eliminate all that do not match.

Here are the answer choices:

6. In lines 24–27, the author most likely uses quotation marks in order to

(A) imply that Vitruvius purposely invented correspondences between proportional measurements of the human body and proportional measurements of the Etruscan temple that he knew didn't exist

(B) underscore the unimportance of Greek philosophy in Vitruvius' treatise

(C) suggest that Vitruvius' background in Greek philosophy prepared him to notice the types of proportional correspondences between the human body and the Etruscan temple he writes about

(D) show that Vitruvius didn't mention proportional correspondences between the human body and the Etruscan temple in his treatise

(E) emphasize Vitruvius' fundamental mistake in his discussion of Etruscan temples

Step 6: Take a moment to double-check your selection.

Guided Practice Explanation: Item 6

Step 1: Cover up the answer choices.

6. In lines 24–27, the author most likely uses quotation marks in order to

Step 2: Read the stem carefully.

This item asks you to get inside the head of the author and explain why he used a particular rhetorical device. In this case, it isn't some highfalutin device like irony or foreshadowing. It's a far more ordinary trope: using quotation marks around a term for a particular rhetorical effect. In our classification, it's closest to a Tone item.

If you were working through a complete set here, you would only attempt this item after you tackled VIC, Main Idea/Purpose, and any other lower-investment items. Always keep Bombing Runs in the back of your mind!

Step 3: If directed to the passage, go back and read the referenced lines.

It's a good idea to quickly review what you already know about this part of the passage and about the passage as a whole. First, we know that this paragraph is about the traditional explanation of Vitruvius' treatment of Etruscan temples. Second, we know that the tone is one of respectful discussion. You've already read a big chunk of this paragraph, but, now that you've been asked a specific question, it makes sense to go back and read the rest.

Step 4: Generate a potential answer *without* looking at the answer choices.

It looks to us like the author put *find* in quotes to let his modern audience know that he, the author, does not share the same Greek philosophical beliefs that he's ascribing to Vitruvius. It's not that he thinks Vitruvius was "making it all up" or being dishonest in any way. The author is simply making sure that his modern audience realizes that he, the author, is keeping his critical distance from Vitruvius. Those two little quotation marks are a very efficient way of saying: "Look, audience, I just want you to know that *I* don't believe in Pythagorean philosophy. But I do want you to realize that *Vitruvius* clearly did, and that belief is the source of the traditional explanation for his treatment of Etruscan temples." We're in the realm of *style* now: how authors use written language to convey their ideas.

Would you have to write out a full paragraph like we just did in order to get this idea straight in your head? Of course not—we're just giving a full explanation. Your jottings might look more like this:

quotes show that V's beliefs not author's

As is the case with most tough reading items, this item turns on how well you can keep the author's beliefs separate from the beliefs of the people the author discusses. In fiction passages, some of the tough items test how well you can keep the narrator's point of view separate from other characters' points of view. That's closely analogous to this kind of common nonfiction item (and it's also another reason why you shouldn't let fiction passages throw you too much). The items are very similar; after all, the SAT wants to test how well you comprehend written material, regardless of whether that material is fiction or nonfiction.

Step 5: Compare your potential fix or answer to the answer choices and eliminate all that do not match.

Here are the answer choices:

6. In lines 24–27, the author most likely uses quotation marks in order to

(A) imply that Vitruvius purposely invented correspondences between proportional   measurements of the human body and proportional measurements of the Etruscan temple that he knew didn't exist

(B) underscore the unimportance of Greek philosophy in Vitruvius' treatise

(C) suggest that Vitruvius' background in Greek philosophy prepared him to notice the types of proportional correspondences between the human body and the Etruscan temple he writes about

(D) show that Vitruvius didn't mention proportional correspondences between the human body and the Etruscan temple in his treatise

(E) emphasize Vitruvius' fundamental mistake in his discussion of Etruscan temples

Look at choice **A**. That's some pretty extreme and harsh language. "Extreme" language isn't just about a few commonly used terms ("all," "every," "none," etc.). It's also a matter of emotion. Answer choices like **A** are usually incorrect, because items test finer distinctions of meaning. If the passage had the tone of an "exposé," then **A** might be correct. But the tone is "respectfully academic." If you were stuck on this item, you could safely eliminate **A** and guess from the rest.

Choice **B** is the opposite of what you want. We know that the author considers the explanation that Greek philosophy shaped Vitruvius' views on architecture to be valid, if incomplete. So **B** can't be correct. Note again how keeping the main idea and purpose of the entire passage and of this chunk in mind helps you weed out the distractors.

Choice **C** looks pretty good. It fits nicely with the main idea and purpose of the passage as a whole and particularly of this chunk of the passage, stating that the use of quotes emphasizes Vitruvius' allegiance to Greek philosophical notions of proportionality while at the same time "announcing" that the author is not claiming some kind of objective truth for these beliefs. All that matters for this argument is that Vitruvius accepted these philosophical beliefs. But don't bubble in **C** yet—always read the other choices.

Choice **D** contradicts the passage. We're told in some detail that Vitruvius did mention these correspondences. Choice **E** shows a misunderstanding of the author's purpose. The author is not out to expose Vitruvius' errors or stupidity. The author is merely reporting what he thinks Vitruvius believed. Whether Vitruvius was right is beside the point. What matters is that Vitruvius thought he was right, and wrote about Etruscan temples accordingly.

These are the kinds of subtle distinctions and nuances of meaning that the tougher RP items test. That's why we've spent so much time working through every decision and consideration: we want to demonstrate how you'll need to think. After some practice, this process will all take place much more quickly.

Step 6: Take a moment to double-check your selection.

Silently read the stem-plus-answer choice to yourself as a check:

> In lines 24–27, the author most likely uses quotation marks in order to suggest that Vitruvius' background in Greek philosophy prepared him to notice the types of proportional correspondences between the human body and the Etruscan temple he writes about.

Guided Practice: Item 7
Now try the following item.

Step 1: Cover up the answer choices.

7. Which of the following, if true, would most clearly strengthen the author's assertion that the introductions to *On Architecture* constitute an ancient résumé (lines 37–47)?

Step 2: Read the stem carefully.

What kind of item is this? Write your answer in the space below:

Step 3: If directed to the passage, go back and read the referenced lines.

Here's the paragraph that contains the referenced lines:

> Despite its title, *On Architecture* was not written primarily for architects. It was written to convince the Emperor Augustus, the most powerful patron in Rome, to give Vitruvius the opportunity to do large-scale architectural work. Vitruvius knew that if Augustus devoted any time at all to *On Architecture*, the emperor would most likely do what busy executives still do to this day: he would read the introductions to each of the ten chapters and skip the rest of the book. Reading *On Architecture* in this manner—each introduction in sequence—is a revelation. One quickly realizes that the chapter introductions constitute an ancient résumé designed to convince Augustus to entrust part of his architectural legacy to Vitruvius.

You may refer back to your margin notes as well. Also, here are our margin notes and notes on main idea, tone, etc.:

First "quarter"	Vitr. and Etruscan temples—why no diversity—why did he simplify in his book? 1st reason: traditional; Greek proportionality
Paragraph 3	another reason—more mundane
Paragraph 4	O.A. not for archs—it's V.'s résumé
Paragraph 5	O.A. originally scrolls, not book
Paragraph 6	résumé + scrolls = another reason for lack of diversity in Et. Temples

Topic	V's book on architecture/Reasons why V. ignored diversity in Etruscan temples
Main Idea	Along with traditional interpretation—V. liked Greek phil.—author adds that purpose of book (to get work for V.) and scroll-nature of book explain lack of diversity.
Purpose	To introduce another "mundane" explanation for why V. ignored diversity in Etruscan temples.
Tone	respectfully academic; a discussion

Step 4: Generate a potential answer *without* looking at the answer choices.

Here's an interesting twist. Is it possible to generate a potential answer to this item? Not really. You know that you need to strengthen the argument, but there are many possible ways to do that.

The key thing to do for items such as this is to make sure you have a clear understanding of what the argument itself is so that you can recognize a strengthener when you see it. So, jot down a restatement of the argument in the space provided below:

Step 5: Compare your potential fix or answer to the answer choices and eliminate all that do not match.

Here are the answer choices:

7. Which of the following, if true, would most clearly strengthen the author's assertion that the introductions to *On Architecture* constitute an ancient résumé (lines 37–47)?

(A) The chapter introductions in *On Architecture* mostly discuss technical matters of architecture.

(B) The chapter introductions of other ancient treatises on architecture tend to advertise their author's qualifications, knowledge, and experience.

(C) The chapter introductions in *On Architecture* consist of a critique of buildings commissioned by Augustus which have already been completed.

(D) The latter portion of each chapter in *On Architecture* contains extended discussion of Vitruvius' various accomplishments and wide-ranging knowledge of architecture.

(E) The chapter introductions in *On Architecture* feature discussions of Vitruvius' qualifications, knowledge, and experience.

Step 6: Take a moment to double-check your selection.

Guided Practice Explanation: Item 7

Step 1: Cover up the answer choices.

7. Which of the following, if true, would most clearly strengthen the author's assertion that the introductions to *On Architecture* constitute an ancient résumé (lines 37–47)?

Step 2: Read the stem carefully.

In our classification, this item is an Inference item. This kind of quick-and-dirty categorization is all that's required. Remember, being able to recognize different types of items is helpful only to the extent that it drives your Bombing-Run decisions.

Specifically, this item tests your understanding of the author's argument by seeing whether you can recognize a way to strengthen that argument. This item also tests your ability to use evidence as support for an argument.

Step 3: If directed to the passage, go back and read the referenced lines.

You may or may not need to do this. How do you know? Well, if you're sure you understand the author's argument, you don't need to look at the passage. If you're understanding is shaky, you should definitely reread it.

Step 4: Generate a potential answer *without* looking at the answer choices.

You will need to look at the choices in this case. So, we'll just mention a particular way of treating items such as these.

Look at this item like an experiment. The argument that the chapter introductions constitute Vitruvius' résumé is the *hypothesis*, and you're looking for data that will support it. With a firm grip on the hypothesis in mind, you're ready to distinguish data that will support it from data that goes against it or simply has no effect on it.

Step 5: Compare your potential fix or answer to the answer choices and eliminate all that do not match.

Here are the answer choices:

7.   Which of the following, if true, would most clearly strengthen the author's assertion that the introductions to *On Architecture* constitute an ancient résumé (lines 37–47)?

(A)   The chapter introductions in *On Architecture* mostly discuss technical matters of architecture.

(B)   The chapter introductions of other ancient treatises on architecture tend to advertise their author's qualifications, knowledge, and experience.

(C)   The chapter introductions in *On Architecture* consist of a critique of buildings commissioned by Augustus which have already been completed.

(D)   The latter portion of each chapter in *On Architecture* contains extended discussion of Vitruvius' various accomplishments and wide-ranging knowledge of architecture.

(E)   The chapter introductions in *On Architecture* feature discussions of Vitruvius' qualifications, knowledge, and experience.

Choice **A** contradicts the hypothesis. If the introductions are a résumé, then you'd expect some résumé-like material to be discussed in the introductions, not technical matters on architecture. Note how the main idea of this paragraph and of the passage as a whole comes into play. The whole point of the résumé argument is that Vitruvius put the most important commission-encouraging information in the introductions because the primary audience was Augustus, not his fellow architects. You would have read this argument when you tackled the passage; it's the first sentence in paragraph four, the paragraph in question in this item. It's safe to eliminate this choice.

Choice **B** is a little tricky. If **B** is true, the best you can say about it is that it's circumstantial evidence: if other ancient architects did this, it's reasonable to infer that Vitruvius did it, too. Does that *most clearly strengthen* the "hypothesis," as the stem asks? Let's read the other choices to find out.

Choice **C** wouldn't help Vitruvius much if the hypothesis that his introductions were his résumé is true. It all depends on how Vitruvius critiqued the buildings. If he wrote his critiques in a way that made them the kind of self-advertisement that our hypothesis maintains the introductions were, then fine. But this choice doesn't actually say that. Not a particularly powerful strengthener, then, is it? It's not as good as **B**, which we're not even all that confident about. So, eliminate **C**.

Choice **D** is kind of the mirror-image of choice **A**. If the introductions are a résumé, then you don't want to bury your résumé material at the *end* of your chapters. This choice can safely be eliminated.

Well, it's either **B** or **E**, right? If, say, you'd spent too much time on this item, you might want to take a guess at this point, having safely eliminated three choices. But let's take a quick peek at **E**.

Hey, wait a minute! This is exactly the kind of data that would most obviously and clearly support the hypothesis given in the stem. Note how you don't have to "help" the answer choice at all, as you did with **B**. This choice does it all by itself, without the need for excessive interpretation.

Step 6: Take a moment to double-check your selection.

In this case, all you need to do is quickly ask yourself, "Do I have all my ducks in a row on this item?" You're set to move on!

Independent Practice: Item 8

After you complete the following item, look at the following page for the explanation. Feel free to refer to your margin notes on the passage, as well as our version of the margin notes and other key features of the passage.

31   Vitruvius' belief that specific natural proportions should be extended to architectural forms does help to explain why he idealized Etruscan temples. After all, mathematical models generally don't allow for much deviation. However, far more mundane considerations acted in concert
35   with Vitruvius' allegiance to Greek notions of mathematical harmony to
36   encourage the idealization of the Etruscan temple.

8.   Which of the following most accurately describes the organization of the third paragraph (lines 31–36)?

(A)   One explanation of a situation is refuted and another is suggested.

(B)   An alternative explanation is supported by evidence.

(C)   An explanation of a situation is determined to be helpful but incomplete.

(D)   An explanation of a situation is used to predict future events.

(E)   Two opposing explanations are reconciled with each other.

Independent Practice Explanation: Item 8

Step 1: Cover up the answer choices.

You did this, right? Don't let those nasty distractors into your head until you're ready.

Step 2: Read the stem carefully.

Items such as these focus on the structure, rather than the content, of arguments in the passage. It's another way of testing whether you have "seen through" the specific information presented to determine how the author deployed that information within the structure of his argument. This is an example of one of the many item subtypes you'll encounter on RPs. We'll refer to it as an Organization item.

From a Bombing-Run point of view, you might have attempted this sooner than other items if you felt confident that you were provided with enough information on this paragraph. Or, you might have decided, "Hey, this paragraph is only three sentences. That won't take long to read." Or, you might have saved it for later, knowing that Organization items are tough for you. The point is to always make judgments on which items will likely be easier for you to handle than others in a given set.

Step 3: If directed to the passage, go back and read the referenced lines.

Here's the third paragraph again:

> Vitruvius' belief that specific natural proportions should be extended to architectural forms does help to explain why he idealized Etruscan temples. After all, mathematical models generally don't allow for much deviation. However, far more mundane considerations acted in concert with Vitruvius' allegiance to Greek notions of mathematical harmony to encourage the idealization of the Etruscan temple.

Step 4: Generate a potential answer *without* looking at the answer choices.

For this item, you can generate a potential answer. Distill the paragraph above down to its essential structure:

Passage Text	Structural Purpose
Vitruvius' belief that specific natural proportions should be extended to architectural forms does help to explain why he idealized Etruscan temples.	Author agrees with traditional explanation.
After all, mathematical models generally don't allow for much deviation.	Support for author's agreement.
However, far more mundane considerations acted in concert with Vitruvius' allegiance to Greek notions of mathematical harmony to encourage the idealization of the Etruscan temple.	Author announces that another kind of explanation exists that complements the traditional explanation.

Of course, we don't want you to actually make a chart like this during the exam. We're just making explicit all of the lightning-quick thoughts and jottings that will go through an experienced test-taker's mind in dealing with this item.

Note how the signpost word *however* marked the "hinge" in the passage, the point at which the author switched from a presentation of "conventional wisdom" to his own explanation. Always be on the lookout for signpost words.

Step 5: Compare your potential fix or answer to the answer choices and eliminate all that do not match.

8. Which of the following most accurately describes the organization of the third paragraph (lines 31–36)?

(A) One explanation of a situation is refuted and another is suggested.

(B) An alternative explanation is supported by evidence.

(C) An explanation of a situation is determined to be helpful but incomplete.

(D) An explanation of a situation is used to predict future events.

(E) Two opposing explanations are reconciled with each other.

Choice **A** is gone: the author does not refute the traditional explanation.

Choice **B** doesn't apply to this paragraph. The author announces that another kind of explanation is possible, but it's more of a complementary explanation than an alternative. What's more, in this paragraph, the author doesn't specifically state what his explanation is, let alone present any evidence for it! **B**'s gone.

Hmmmm . . . **C** looks pretty good. Let's check the other two, though, just to be sure.

Choice **D** is the left-field choice. No prediction is made. Eliminate.

Choice **E** is a distortion. First, the two explanations are clearly presented as complementary, not mutually exclusive. Second, no attempt is made to reconcile the two positions. The second explanation has yet to be specifically stated, and the author clearly doesn't see the need for "reconciliation" because the arguments are not in conflict with each other. Eliminate choice **E**. **C** it is!

See how having some idea of what the correct answer should be saves time? You can simply run through the choices and eliminate those that are incorrect, rather than constantly jumping between each answer choice and the relevant part of the passage over and over again.

Step 6: Take a moment to double-check your selection.

Again, pause for a split second to make sure your answer choice is correct.

SECTION-LEVEL STRATEGIES

You're now familiar with how SAT Reading Passages are constructed. Items come in sets that are associated with a particular passage or passages. You've learned separate step methods that govern how to tackle:

- The **passage** itself.
- The **set** of items associated with that passage (i.e., Bombing Runs).
- Each individual **item** in the set.

There's another "level" to this passage-set-item hierarchy, however. RPs come in test **sections**. In the case of RPs, the section is called Critical Reading. Any given SAT test will consist of at least two Critical Reading sections. These sections may contain any of the following elements:

- Some number of Sentence Completions
- Some number of short RPs, including, possibly, a short paired RP
- One or more long RPs
- A paired RP

Furthermore, the passages mentioned may be on any of the following topics:

- Fiction
- Humanities
- Social Science
- Science

Remember the cardinal rule of standardized test-taking: since all items are worth the same number of points, *always* do those items you find easiest first. In other words:

Always fly Bombing Runs.

We're now extending the concept of Bombing Runs to the section level, applying it to *passages* and *item types* as well as to individual items within any given passage set.

For example, let's assume you see a section composed of the following items and sets in the following order:

- 10 Sentence Completions
- 2 short RPs, one on a scientific topic, and one on a topic from the humanities
- 2 long RPs, one social science and one science

Here's how you'd fly a Bombing Run on this section:

- Do the Sentence Completions first. They require a far lower time investment than any reading items.
- Next, tackle the short RPs. They require less of an investment than the long passages. If you're into science, do that one first. If not, do the humanities one first.
- Tackle whichever long RP you think will be easier to handle. Length may play a role—long passages can vary from 400 to 800 or more words. Topic may also determine your selection: science heads will likely jump on the science passage set first.
- If you have time, work on the remaining long RP.

Within each set you attempt, you'll decide which items you'll attempt first and which you'll leave for last.

Making these types of judgments requires a bit of self-knowledge and practice. But that investment pays off many times over. Picture two identical test-takers. They each have exactly the same level of knowledge and skills. They each follow all the strategies presented in this book, with one critical exception. One flies Bombing Runs, jumping around the section in an intelligent fashion and racking up all the "easy" points she can as quickly as possible. The other one just starts with the first item and works his way through the section without skipping around. Which test-taker is going to get a higher score? Which test-taker will be judged *less* able, despite the fact that both test-takers have *identical* knowledge and skills?

You want to maximize your score by distributing your knowledge across a section as efficiently as possible. Flying Bombing Runs ensures that this distribution will happen.

THE 11 MOST COMMON MISTAKES

As you prepare, keep the following common mistakes in mind. Some are mistakes to avoid when taking the actual test; others are mistakes to avoid during your preparation for the test. Some apply to all item- and passage-types; others are more specific.

1. Reading long RPs word-for-word/refusing to skim. Maximize the time you spend on the items. Answering items correctly is what gets you points.

2. Reading passively. Make margin notes; mark up the passage; have a sense of what each chunk of the passage, as well as the passage as a whole is about.

3. Looking at the answer choices without having some idea of what the correct answer should be. If at all possible, make sure you come up with your own answer first so you're not at the mercy of the distractors.

4. Spending too much time (more than a minute or so) on any one item in a set.

5. Failing to practice the step methods on every practice RP set—*reading* the book is not enough!

6. Refusing to guess when you've eliminated one answer choice.

7. Refusing to fly Bombing Runs on items. That is, refusing to do a passage's items out of order based on your judgment of which will be easier and yield points more quickly.

8. Refusing to fly Bombing Runs on passages. That is, refusing to attempt passage sets out of order based on your judgment of which will be easier and yield points more quickly.

9. Refusing to fly Bombing Runs on sections. That is, refusing to work first on those passage types or item types that will yield points more quickly. Specifically, do the Sentence Completions first, then short RPs, and then long RPs/paired RPs.

10. In Paired RPs: Reading both passages and then attempting all the items. Tackle one passage first. Then tackle that passage's items. Next, tackle the other passage. Then tackle that passage's items. If you have time, attempt the compare-and-contrast items.

11. Not taking advantage of Backward Strategies when you're stuck.

CONCLUSION

THE IMPORTANCE OF PRACTICING EARNESTLY

Much of what you've learned is intuitive, but some of it, like Bombing Runs and skimming, is not. No matter how much attention you've paid thus far, unless you complete your training by following the step methods we've presented, you're putting an artificial ceiling on your ultimate score. Don't do that! Achieve your potential; maximize your score.

Let's face it: handling RPs is tough. You have a lot to keep in mind, so we encourage you to keep your practice sessions short and intense. You'll need to get used to maintaining a very high level of concentration in order to maximize your score on RPs, so don't burn yourself out.

Without practice, you won't master RPs. You've learned quite a bit since you picked up this little book, but now comes the hard part—*you* have to apply it to testlike items. You'll find several practice sets at the end of this book. Here are some tips for getting the most out of these items:

- **Do not time yourself on the first few reading passage sets.** When you begin, don't worry about time at all. Take as long as you need to work through each set.

- **Read the explanations for all items, regardless of whether you got them right or wrong.** This last part is critical—always read *all* the explanations for each set's items. The idea is to develop skills that will help you score points as quickly as possible. Most important, scoring a point doesn't mean you got it in the most efficient manner. The overarching goal is to *apply* the methods you've learned. Whether you get all, some, or none of the practice items right doesn't matter.

After the first set, you may want to start paying attention to time. Certainly, by the actual test, give yourself about a minute or so per item.

ADDITIONAL ONLINE PRACTICE

Once you're done working through the items and explanations in this book, you can practice further by going online to **testprep.sparknotes.com** and taking full-length SAT tests. These practice tests provide you with instant feedback, delineating all your strengths and weaknesses.

Also, be sure to take the free reading passages posttest to see how well you've absorbed the content of this book. For this posttest, go to **testprep.sparknotes.com/powertactics**.

OTHER WAYS TO PREPARE

If you are not a reader, become one. Reading high-quality prose and learning by example is one of the most important (and pleasant!) ways to become a good writer. Read literary fiction and magazines or newspapers with high-quality writing, such as the *New York Times*, the *Wall Street Journal*, *Scientific American*, *Harper's*, the *Atlantic Monthly*, the *Nation*, and the *Economist*. Many of these publications are available for free on the Internet. The literary fiction you're reading in school will also help prepare you for fiction RPs.

Keep in mind that almost all fiction passages are from twentieth-century literature, although some excerpts may be taken from the late nineteenth century. While reading Shakespeare is in general a very good idea, it won't match the type of fiction you'll most likely see on the SAT. George Orwell or Ernest Hemingway would be a better bet. Furthermore, the fiction is conventional, not experimental. If you'd like to tackle some James Joyce, you'll find far more SAT-relevant prose in his short-story collection *Dubliners* than in his later experimental works *Ulysses* and *Finnegans Wake*. RPs aren't a test of esoteric literature or literary criticism. They're a test of your ability to comprehend conventional prose.

On to the practice sets!

THE PRACTICE
SETS

LONG READING PASSAGE: FICTION

Questions 1–9 refer to the passage below.

The following passage is from a 2003 novel about a young woman named Angela who at age eight left China with her family to move to San Francisco.

Our parents had known each other in China; we'd even taken the same boat to America. However, within five years of our arrival in San Francisco, Norman and I had become strangers. Relatives already established in the city helped Norman's parents assimilate. Within a

5   year, they had not only learned English, but had also become real estate moguls. I learned all this from the Chinese American gossip machine that constantly tabulated every family's level of success. The machine judged my family lacking. My parents ran a grocery store and, unlike Norman's family, gravitated to the immigrant subculture. They never

10 learned English, but they respected that I tamed that beast of a language. I was my parents' communication link with the "outside world."

     My parents denied themselves in order to ensure that I could attend Baywood, a top private high school. That was where Norman and I

15 crossed paths again. However much my relative mastery of English had elevated my status at home, at Baywood I remained a shy and brainy outsider. Norman was very popular: he played football and was elected class president. He and gorgeous Judy Kim were named King and Queen of the Winter Ball; their portrait adorned every available bulletin

20 board. I scoffed at the celebrity silently. Back then, I did everything silently. Compared to Norman, who had already achieved the American teenage ideal, I was anonymous. From the sidelines I observed his triumphs with barely acknowledged envy.

     In May of our freshman year, Norman approached me after our

25 chemistry class.

"Hey, Angela," he said as my heart leapt into my throat. "I missed class a couple of days ago. Can I copy your notes?"

"Sure," I said. I was horrified to find myself blushing.

We soon became study buddies. It was all business—no small talk beyond the necessary niceties. But the hours we piled up studying together generated an unspoken mutual respect and an unacknowledged intimacy. Judy noticed this and took an increasing dislike to me. This relationship continued throughout high school.

One day in eleventh grade, without looking up from the math problem he was working on, Norman asked: "What schools are you applying to?"

It was the first time he had shown any real personal interest in me. "Berkeley, if I'm lucky," I said.

"You could probably get in anywhere."

"What do you mean?"

He looked up from his math problem and met my gaze.

"Berkeley is just across the bay. Don't you want to experience something new for once? I'm applying to schools back East," he said. "You should, too."

Not for the first time, an exciting vision of ivy-covered walls and perhaps even a new identity swept over me and was almost immediately subsumed by a wave of guilt.

"But what about my parents?"

"But what about *you*?"

Norman had broken a taboo. I launched into a self-righteous refutation of the possibility he had dared to voice. I told him that even though *I* wasn't popular and *my* family wasn't as successful as his, *I* at least hadn't forgotten that it was my parents who had brought me here and who had struggled so much for me. How could I make them unhappy?

Norman had expected this outburst. He smiled. "We're not so different, you know. We started out in the same boat. Now we're in the same boat again." He laughed. "We've always been in the same boat. Our parents might be kind of different, but they want us to succeed and be happy."

"You're so American," I said in a tone hovering between approval and reproach. "You're not even worried about leaving your parents to go to school back East."

"That's not what being American means," he insisted.

"Well, what does it mean, then?" I demanded. Surely, I, and not this superficial football player who needed my academic help, knew what it meant to be American. That very day I had received an A on my American History term paper.

70   "It means, Angela," he said gently, "that our parents brought us here
so we could have the freedom to figure out *for ourselves* what to do with
our lives."

He smiled at my speechlessness and then returned to his math
problem.

Without looking up from his notebook, he said, "If I can decide to go to
75   school back East, so can you."

1.   What is the purpose of the information in the first sentence?

    (A) to show Angela and Norman's similar histories so as to
          emphasize their current differences
    (B) to emphasize that both Angela and Norman have come a
          long way since their childhoods in China
    (C) to let the reader know that Angela came from a poor family
          that could not afford to fly to America
    (D) to make the reader think that Norman and Angela will
          inevitably become friends
    (E) to let the reader see how highly Angela values her family's
          history

2.   The word "tabulated" in line 7 emphasizes that

    (A) the other Chinese immigrants were very aware of who was
          succeeding in a material way and who was not
    (B) Angela's neighbors calculated the exact amount of money
          her family was earning
    (C) Norman's family checked the prices of everything they
          owned
    (D) Angela lived in a poor section of San Francisco
    (E) Angela was determined to earn more money than Norman

3.   The use of italics in line 49 serves to emphasize

    (A) Norman's unrealistic desire to go to school outside of
          California
    (B) Norman's idealistic goals as contrasted with Angela's lack of
          ambition
    (C) Norman's concern that Angela has not thought about her
          own educational desires
    (D) the small chance that Angela will accomplish her dreams
    (E) the degree to which Angela has undermined her potential

4. Angela's response in lines 50–55 reveals that she

    (A) wants Norman to be impressed with her
    (B) is afraid to express her true emotions
    (C) stubbornly wants to attend Berkeley
    (D) is unable to reveal her true ambitions to Norman
    (E) has consistently adopted her parents' happiness as her own

5. In line 61, Angela uses the word "American" to differentiate between

    (A) concern for the future and fear of failure
    (B) personal ambition and responsibility to one's parents
    (C) imagination and conservatism
    (D) duty to family and duty to friends
    (E) love for adventure and love for travel

6. In lines 67–68, Angela mentions her A on her history paper in order to

    (A) suggest that she assumes that she knows the definition of
        "American" better than Norman
    (B) emphasize the high quality of her education
    (C) highlight the irony of knowing the textbook definition of a
        term versus a real-life meaning
    (D) remind herself that she has spent many years mastering the
        English language
    (E) strengthen her resolve to go to school in Berkeley instead of
        the East Coast

7. Norman's statement in lines 69–71 primarily shows him to be

    (A) selfish in his desires to achieve success
    (B) ambitious in a manner Angela had not considered for herself
    (C) dismissive of his parents' hopes for his future
    (D) secretly hoping to corrupt Angela's future plans
    (E) arrogant in overestimating his abilities

8. Throughout the passage, the main focus is on

   (A) the awkwardness Angela feels knowing that Norman already has a girlfriend

   (B) Angela's ambition to do well in school and get into a good college

   (C) the challenges Angela faces living in America while feeling like an outsider

   (D) Angela's excitement over getting an A on her history term paper

   (E) how personal ambition is the key to getting ahead in America

9. From details in the passage, it is clear that

   (A) Angela went ahead with her plan to attend Berkeley

   (B) Angela grew to be more outspoken

   (C) Norman went on to play football in college

   (D) Angela decided to go to college back East

   (E) Angela majored in math at college

LONG READING PASSAGE: FICTION— ANSWERS & EXPLANATIONS

1. A

The first sentence informs the reader that Angela's parents and Norman's parents knew each other in China and that the two young people came across on the same boat. This common history contrasts with and thereby draws attention to their very different personalities and very different attitudes toward their family responsibilities and personal ambitions: Norman is popular and wants to explore America, while Angela is shy and wants to stay close to home. These differences provide the passage with its tension and interest. The other answers all offer details that may be true to a certain extent, but none of which is as important to the passage as a whole.

2. A

The word *tabulated* appears in the passage to express what the "Chinese American gossip machine" does with regard to "every family's success," and from the context of the passage it is clear that this involves keeping a record of that success and comparing it to the success of other Chinese American families, things for which one might use a table or chart. Choice **B** is tempting since the word *tabulated* sounds like and is occasionally used to mean "calculated," but it is clear that in this context comparisons of status are more germane than exact calculations of salaries.

3.   **C**

Angela responds to Norman's suggestion that she think about applying to East Coast colleges with the question "What about my parents?" because she thinks it would be wrong to move far away from her mother and father. Norman, however, thinks it would be worse for Angela to put concern for her parents ahead of her own educational ambitions, and the word *you* is italicized to express his desire that Angela should consider her own interests first.

4.   **E**

Angela's answer to Norman's question "What about *you*?" hinges on the idea that she has not forgotten that her parents brought her to America and provided her with the opportunity to excel there. As a result, she feels that she can be happy if and only if her parents are happy. This is clearly articulated by the final part of her response: "How could I make them unhappy?"

5.   **B**

Angela clarifies her remark that Norman is "so American" by telling him, "You're not even worried about leaving your parents to go to school back East." Angela is shocked that Norman would put his personal ambition (to attend an Eastern college) before his responsibilities to his parents (which would entail going to school close to their home on the West Coast).

6.   **A**

Angela has accused Norman of being "so American" for not worrying about leaving his parents behind to attend college on the East Coast, and he has replied by challenging her definition of "being American." Angela mentions the high grade she received on her paper to suggest that her definition *has* to be better than Norman's since she considers herself to be smarter than he. Choice **B** is attractive since getting an A on a paper seems to relate to the idea of being well educated, but Angela is not concerned with the quality of the education she has received, only the fact that she considers herself intellectually superior to Norman. Similarly, choice **C** is tempting because the word "textbook" seems to fit with a school grade, but Angela's comment is not concerned with the distinctions between textbook and real-life definitions. Rather, it shows that she assumes herself to be intellectually superior to her study-buddy, Norman.

7. **B**

Norman's statement expresses his opinion that his parents want him to do whatever he thinks is best for himself and the fact that he is keen to embrace such freedom. This attitude is in marked contrast to Angela's, which only extends to personal ambitions that coincide with her parents' interests. Choice **A** is tempting since at the time the story takes place, Angela clearly thinks such self-interest is selfish. But this is not Norman's belief. Choice **C** is attractive for the same reason. Choice **D** is too extreme—Norman is trying to help Angela, as Angela has helped him with his studies.

8. **C**

The main idea of the first paragraph is that Angela's family never assimilated into American culture the way Norman's did, and was even judged as insufficient by the "Chinese American gossip machine." In the second paragraph, the reader learns that Angela felt like an outsider at high school, despite her success in learning English. Finally, in the conversation with Norman, Angela realizes that her study partner may know more about what it means to be American, regardless of the A she got on her American History paper, and that she has never considered taking advantage of the freedom to choose that her parents provided her by bringing her to America. Throughout the passage, Angela feels that she is alienated from her surroundings in one way or another. The other choices are details of the passage, or distortions of those details.

9. **B**

Remember, *Angela*—an older, wiser Angela—is the narrator. In lines 20–21, Angela remarks that "back then, I did everything silently." The phrase *back then* indicates that doing everything silently is something

Angela overcame later in life and that she became more outspoken. Although Norman's suggestion that she could attend an Eastern college clearly made an impact on Angela, it is not clear from the passage whether she decided to follow up on this idea or stick with her plan to attend Berkeley, so answers **A** and **D** are incorrect. There is no indication that Angela went on to major in math or that Norman continued to play football, so answers **C** and **E** are incorrect.

PAIRED READING PASSAGE: SCIENCE

<u>Directions:</u> *The passages below are followed by questions based on the content of the passages and the relationship between the two passages. Answer the questions on the basis of what the passage* <u>states</u> *or* <u>implies</u> *and on any introductory material provided.*

<u>Questions 1–12</u> refer to the following pair of passages.

On January 14, 2004, President Bush announced a reorganization of NASA resources to make a manned mission to Mars the agency's primary goal. This announcement reignited a long-smoldering debate on manned space travel. These passages, adapted from recently published articles, discuss the advisability of further American investment in manned space travel.

Passage 1

The popularity of manned space flight stems from a peculiar mixture of American ideals buried deep in the national consciousness. Can-do optimism and engineering know-how combine with a New Frontier to provide something quasi-religious: the chance to be born again by
5   ascending to the heavens. Unprecedented material benefits—the storied "spin-offs" that we're always promised—will doubtlessly emanate from this noble effort that will unify our fractious country. Marshalling America's techno-scientific expertise for a Pilgrimage into space will allow us to re-enact our national origins and renew our appointed role:
10   to create a shining City on a Hill in a New World that presents the last best hope of mankind. Thus, manned space flight reconciles seemingly contradictory aspects of the national identity: nostalgic and forward-looking, religious and scientific, spiritual and material.

    Only through the sobering examination of the costs and benefits of
15   manned space flight can the effect of so seductively romantic a brew be shaken off. Should we spend hundreds of billions of dollars on, say, a

mission to Mars when we face crushing problems such as poverty, terrorism, and global warming? The likely benefits of manned space flight had better be staggering in the face of the opportunity costs* of not directly investing in problems such as these.

Thus, I would like to discuss a non-romantic argument often put forth in favor of manned space flight. Enthusiasts claim that space-based scientific research is both invaluable and impossible to replicate on Earth. There is little proof for this claim. For example, *Mir*, the now-defunct space station, yielded no scientific breakthroughs commensurate with its cost. In one experiment, scientists concluded that plants did not grow well in space. Clearly, this bit of information would be invaluable only to astronauts. Furthermore, a reexamination of this experiment found that plant growth had been stunted for quite mundane and well-understood reasons. Ethylene, a gas long known to be released by plants, had accumulated in the enclosure and inhibited growth. So much for invaluable groundbreaking advances. As for important research that can't be accomplished on Earth, it is often argued that the only way to study the long-term effects of zero-gravity on the human body is in space. This argument carries weight only for those already committed to manned space flight. But as an independent argument *for* manned space flight, this argument is circular: we must have manned space flight to understand the long-term effects of zero-gravity in order to have more manned space flight.

A sober cost/benefit analysis shows that robotic space exploration trumps manned space flight. Robots have proven to be remarkably effective at exploring our solar system. Their scientific impact is ubiquitously acknowledged. In terms of financial and human cost, robot expeditions are far cheaper to mount.

The circularity of even seemingly non-romantic arguments for manned space flight belies the fundamental romanticism of its supporters. Doubtlessly unaware of the ingredients in the seductive brew noted above, enthusiasts support manned space flight because they think it would be really fun and exciting. Being an American, I can understand this. I, too, yearn for adventures on alien shores. But even though it would be really fun and exciting to deplete all my savings on a year-long adventure on merely Mediterranean shores, as an adult I know that I have more pressing, if less enticing, claims on my resources. Those who argue for manned space flight do so out of romantic, escapist, and childlike notions that they should outgrow.

* An "opportunity cost" is a comparison between the likely return on one investment and the likely return on another.

Passage 2

The orbiting astronaut looks down on his home and grasps both its fragility and the pettiness of our mundane conflicts. How trite! How dare we spend vast sums on manned space flight when six billion of us live in the midst of conflicts and problems, which, while perhaps "petty" from a 60 God's-eye view, threaten the future of our civilization and species? Furthermore, the oft-made assertion that manned space experiments have yielded critical advances either directly or indirectly is arguable at best.

So goes the fashionable critique of manned space travel. However, 65 rather than cynically dismiss the astronaut's now proverbial reaction to seeing the Earth from on high, I propose that we consider the potential benefits that this change in perspective would have on real-world problems were it only spread more widely. Moreover, equally intangible "romantic" impulses to explore should not be thrown aside so lightly. 70 Motivation matters. Where would we be today if Christopher Columbus had not embarked on his "folly" to open a western passage to the East? Beneficial unintended consequences—or, "spin-offs"—are real and pre-date the moon shot. Columbus, in fact, failed to open a new trade route to the East, but he did find two continents previously unknown to his 75 contemporaries in Europe, Asia, and Africa. While clearly not entirely beneficial—especially for the millions of Native Americans felled by Old-World diseases or conquistadors' muskets—Columbus' discovery nevertheless made great things possible, such as the United States.

Rather than retreat in embarrassment from the charge of 80 "romanticism," we should embrace it. The case for manned space flight should rest explicitly upon the rejuvenating and unifying potential the effort provides our troubled world. In particular, we should cease insisting that immensely important scientific discoveries are imminent and inevitable. While this almost certainly is the case, we really don't 85 need *manned* space flight to yield scientific discoveries; robots do very well for that purpose. Moreover, the real-world benefits of intangible inspiration are not limited to a welcome and fruitful change in perspective. How many young people would rush into the sciences if a full-scale global effort in manned space flight—a mission to Mars is the 90 obvious choice—were launched? How beneficial would the consequences of the requisite and unprecedented international cooperation be for the grave issues that face our species here on Earth?

Rather than promise dubious economic boons when we're labeled "escapist," we should explicitly state the possibility that we have already 95 failed on this planet and that space is our only long-term option. Most scientists agree that we are already dangerously close to Earth's carrying capacity. Surely, within the half-century or so it would take to truly conquer manned space flight, we will be that much closer to a nightmare of ecological or societal collapse. Doesn't the likely prospect of global collapse in itself represent the most massive opportunity cost possible for *not* investing heavily in manned space flight? It's at the very least arguable that the new frontier of the Americas gave rise to a kind of society whose ideals truly are the last best hope of mankind. Wouldn't the new frontier of space bestow another opportunity for fruitful experiments in enlightened government? I maintain that we cannot afford to throw aside the undeniable romantic appeal that a global effort to put man in space would engender. Our civilization will need all the help it can get to survive this century. I can think of no argument for manned space flight more unromantic than that.

1. Which of the following, if true, would most clearly STRENGTHEN the assertion in Passage 1 about science experiments conducted in space (lines 25–31)?

    (A) Many of the recent developments in gene therapy are directly attributed to experiments conducted on *Mir*.

    (B) Recent reports have questioned the objectivity of the critics of the *Mir* program.

    (C) A full report on all experiments conducted in space has yet to be evaluated.

    (D) A list of the 100 most important scientific discoveries since the beginning of manned space travel yielded none based on experiments conducted in space.

    (E) Many of the experiments conducted in space are highly technical, and not easily accessible to the layman.

2.   With which of the following statements would the author of Passage 1 be LEAST likely to agree?

(A) When considering whether an investment is worthwhile, the likely benefits of that investment should be weighed against the likely benefits of a similar investment in another venture.

(B) The benefits of manned space missions do not outweigh the benefits of robotic space missions to a degree significant enough to justify the higher cost of the former.

(C) The strong support for manned space missions among Americans is surprising given the spirituality of the American people.

(D) It is part of the American character to be attracted by the idea of experiencing exciting adventures in new territories.

(E) Part of becoming an adult is coming to recognize that the potential benefits of any venture must be weighed against the costs.

3.   In the context of lines 36–39, the reference to "circular" serves to

(A) outline the path which astronauts take when in orbit

(B) emphasize that arguments which support sending humans into space are self-serving

(C) illustrate the accuracy needed to gauge an astronaut's health in space

(D) demonstrate the progress that has been made in helping humans to adapt to the demands of space

(E) refute the argument that space travel is costly and even unnecessary

4.   In line 41, "trumps" most nearly means

(A) devises

(B) suits

(C) duplicates

(D) outperforms

(E) defrauds

5.   According to Passage 2, the argument that people should not go into space is

(A) harmlessly entertaining
(B) unjustly scornful
(C) logically flawed
(D) astutely argued
(E) unnecessarily complicated

6.   The author of Passage 2 begins by describing an astronaut's view from space in order to

(A) emphasize that the astronaut is a kind of national hero
(B) show how overly simplistic things look in space
(C) prepare the reader for the idea that new perspectives can be important
(D) warn the reader against adopting an overly romantic notion of space travel
(E) prove that environmental problems are so severe that their effects can be seen from space

7.   The word "fashionable" in line 64 most nearly means

(A) flattering
(B) apparent
(C) wholesome
(D) trendy
(E) conspicuous

8.   Which of the following strategies for arguing in favor of manned space missions would the author of Passage 2 be MOST likely to favor?

(A) emphasizing the importance of scientific experiments conducted in space
(B) showing the benefits of traveling to Mars
(C) emphasizing the way it will nurture and inspire positive sentiments in the people back on Earth
(D) proving precisely what discoveries lie in wait for us in space
(E) eliminating the danger of manned space travel

9. Which of the following most accurately describes the last paragraph of Passage 2 in relation to arguments in Passage 1?

(A) The author of Passage 2 proposes a new argument and revives an argument dismissed in Passage 1.

(B) The author of Passage 2 predicts a future series of events also considered in Passage 1.

(C) The author of Passage 2 examines an idea from Passage 1 and disputes the figures offered in support.

(D) The author of Passage 2 asserts a viewpoint shared by the author of Passage 1 by offering up historical evidence.

(E) The author of Passage 2 reconciles his point of view with the author of Passage 1.

10. In each passage, the author assumes that the efficacy of scientific experiments conducted in space is

(A) useful only if carefully monitored by a mirror crew on the ground

(B) called into question only by the most cynical of observers

(C) tragically underutilized by the most talented scientists

(D) only justifiable under certain circumstances

(E) not enough to justify manned space flight

11. The passages differ in their evaluation of manned space flight in that Passage 1 claims that

(A) space enthusiasts ultimately want to go to the moon for romantic notions

(B) propagandists have falsified the data of scientific experiments to justify their continued use

(C) the only real benefits of manned space travel could be achieved less expensively with robotic space exploration

(D) Christopher Columbus had a specific goal in mind when he set off on his journey

(E) the only way to understand the long-term impact of space travel on the body is to engage in manned space flights

12. Both passages are primarily concerned with

(A) the poor planning of current space missions

(B) the future of manned space flight

(C) the eventuality of going to Mars

(D) the best way to improve the space program

(E) the introduction of more math and science into the school curriculum

PAIRED READING PASSAGES: SCIENCE— ANSWERS & EXPLANATIONS

1. **D**

Passage 1 asserts that scientific experiments conducted in space do not yield results important enough to offset their costs, so the correct answer will offer an argument supporting this idea. If it were true that none of the 100 most important scientific discoveries since the beginning of manned space travel was conducted in space, this fact would certainly strengthen the position presented in the first passage. The other answers are incorrect because they all offer facts that, if true, would weaken the claim that scientific experiments conducted in space are not worth their costs.

2. **C**

In lines 2–5, the author of Passage 1 asserts that the idea of sending people into space to explore new frontiers is "quasi-religious" and appeals to the desire to be born again in the heavens; the author seems convinced that the spirituality of Americans is one of the driving forces behind support for the space program. The other answers all offer statements with which the author of Passage 1 would certainly agree, given details and arguments in the passage.

3. **B**

In the third paragraph, the author of Passage 1 shows how the experiments performed aboard the *Mir* space station yielded findings that can only be of use in future manned space missions. In other words, one of the main arguments used to support the continuation of manned missions is based on the assumption that such a continuation will be granted. The argument is self-serving because it essentially says that manned space missions are necessary because manned space missions require research performed on manned space missions.

4. **D**

In the context of the passage, the word *trumps* is being used to describe the way robotic space exploration is more effective than or *outperforms* manned space flight. None of the words offered in the other answer choices makes sense in the context of the passage. **A** and **E** offer clearly nonsensical definitions. **B**, *suits*, does not make sense since robotic and manned space flights are alternatives to one another—a mission is either robotic *or* manned, so one cannot *suit* the other. **C** is more logical, but it would not be accurate to say that robotic space missions *duplicate* manned ones since the author has just asserted that the scientific accomplishments of the former are universally recognized while those of the latter are only important to astronauts.

5.   **B**

The abrasive language the author uses to articulate the argument against manned space travel ("How trite! How dare we...?"), and the fact that the reader is cautioned against "cynically" dismissing the astronaut's perspective indicate that this argument is regarded as being *unjustly scornful*. **C**, *logically flawed*, is tempting, but Passage 2 disputes the logic against manned space travel showing that supposedly "romantic" arguments in favor of it are actually morbidly hard-headed: "Our civilization will need all the help it can get to survive this century. I can think of no argument for manned space flight more unromantic than that." There is no evidence to suggest that any of the assessments offered by the other answer choices is accurate.

6.   **C**

In the second paragraph, the author expresses the idea that the astronaut's experience of seeing the Earth from space grants a new perspective on earthly affairs that might be beneficial if it were spread more widely across the population. **B** and **D** are both tempting because within the first paragraph it appears that the author is criticizing the importance people attach to the astronaut's unique view of the world. Reading the paragraph in the context of the entire passage reveals that the author is writing ironically, however, and is actually objecting to the way people tend to scoff at this enlightening experience.

7.   **D**

The word *fashionable* is applied to the prevailing view of manned space travel against which the author of Passage 2 is arguing. This view is obviously popular at the time of writing (otherwise the author would not need to address it), so *trendy* is the best meaning. *Flattering* is incorrect since the prevailing view is clearly negative, and *apparent, wholesome,* or *conspicuous* do not make sense in context.

8. **C**

At the end of the first paragraph of Passage 2, the author acknowledges that the scientific benefits of manned space missions are debatable. The next paragraph counters this point by arguing that manned space flights are the product of an impulse to explore, which should be nurtured, given that it led to the discovery of the Americas, and the third paragraph asserts that such missions would foster beneficial sentiments of curiosity and cooperativeness. The author clearly sees nurturing and inspiring positive sentiments as among the greatest benefits of manned space flight. The other answers are incorrect because they either contradict the argument of the passage (in the case of **A**) or deal with details not considered in the passage (as in the case of **B**, **D**, and **E**).

9. **A**

In the final paragraph, the author of Passage 2 introduces the new argument that manned space travel may become essential as life on Earth becomes unbearable, and then makes a case for the idea (dismissed in Passage 1 when the author describes how to "shake off" the effects of the "romantic brew") that the creation of a New Frontier will provide opportunities for social experimentation and hope for enlightened government. **B** is tempting since the author does predict societal and environmental collapse, but this situation is not considered in Passage 1. **D** is also attractive since the author refers to early American history, but the relevant idea about the New Frontier is clearly not shared by the author of the first passage. The author of Passage 2 neither disputes figures offered in Passage 1 (there is none to dispute) nor reconciles his viewpoint with that of its author, so **C** and **E** are incorrect.

10. **E**

The author of Passage 1 argues extensively for the idea that the scientific discoveries of manned space missions are only useful for future manned space missions, and the author of Passage 2, who proposes other benefits, nevertheless does nothing to refute the idea that the scientific advances yielded by manned space experiments are "arguable at best." None of the other answers offers an opinion expressed by either author.

11. **C**

The question asks for a way in which the passages differ in their evaluation of manned space flight, so the right answer must offer a distinction between the two passages that has a bearing on their differing stances regarding sending people into space. **C** is the only answer which meets this requirement—the author of the first passage dismisses the romantic benefits of manned space travel and notes that the scientific benefits can be realized by robotic missions at a lower cost. **A** looks attractive at first since criticism of the romantic nature of support for manned space flight is a major element in the first passage's argument; however, both passages acknowledge that there are romantic motivations behind manned space travel, and the second passage merely differs by understanding this as a good thing rather than a problem. **B** is incorrect because the author of Passage 1 never claims that the scientific findings were falsified, merely that they are only relevant to further manned missions. **D** is incorrect because Columbus is only mentioned in the second passage. **E** is incorrect because only the first passage mentions the impact of space travel on humans, and actually dismisses it as being of use only to future manned space missions.

12. **B**

Both passages focus on arguments concerning the future of manned space flight. Note that both passages draw a distinction between manned and unmanned missions to space. **A** is incorrect because neither passage criticizes the planning of current space missions, though the first passage questions the need for those missions which carry humans into space. **C** and **E** are incorrect because they offer details from the passages, not their shared focus. **D** is incorrect because both passages are focused on one specific aspect of the space program—manned missions, and not the space program in general. This answer is too broad.

LONG READING PASSAGE: SOCIAL SCIENCE

Questions 1–10 below are based on the following passage.

The following excerpt was taken from an article on the role of the Electoral College in presidential elections.

In 2000, for the first time in 112 years, the candidate who won the popular vote did not become president. This event underscored a curious fact about our political system. Strictly speaking, American voters do not elect their president. A group of people collectively referred to as the Electoral College elects the president on behalf of the American people. How did this strange institution come to be?

Two critical and interlocking concerns shaped how the founders structured the Electoral College. First, the founders wanted to put a check on the popular will. The United States was to be a republic, not a democracy. To the founders, "democracy" meant mob rule. The founders had been horrified by Shays' rebellion in Massachusetts, in which impoverished farmers took up arms against their creditors. By preventing direct popular election of the chief executive, the framers hoped to prevent an American Caesar from destroying the republic by playing on the easily swayed will of the ignorant and unpropertied masses.

Second, the Electoral College was intended to balance the power of large and small states to choose the chief executive. Such a balance had been struck in the legislative branch: the Senate had equal state representation, whereas the House of Representatives featured proportional state representation. Large states had more influence in the House, but all states had equal influence in the Senate. Analogously, the framers empowered state legislatures to appoint or select several

electors, the number of which was to equal the sum of that state's
25   representatives and two senators. On a day decreed by Congress, all
electors were to meet in their respective states and cast ballots for the
presidency. A list recording all votes was to be signed, certified, sealed,
and delivered to the president of the Senate (i.e., the vice president of
the United States). In a joint session of Congress, the president of the
30   Senate was to unseal and count the votes from all the states. Whichever
candidate garnered the most votes became the president-elect, as long
as he had a majority of all votes cast. The runner-up became the vice
president-elect.

These rules forced the Constitution's framers to take some special
35   cases into account. In the event that two candidates split the Electoral
College evenly, both would have a majority, but neither would have the
most votes. The election would then go to the House, where each state's
delegation would cast a single vote for president. In the event that no
candidate carried a majority, the House's state delegations would choose
40   from among the top five vote-getters. In either case, the runner-up in the
House election would become vice president. (In the case of a tie for
second place, the Senate would vote for one of the two candidates.) The
rules by which these contingencies were to be adjudicated demonstrate
the founders' desire to balance the power of large and small states. The
45   founders expected that large states would in effect determine who the
"candidates" for president were, but small and large states would have
an equal say in which candidate ultimately became president.

For all their concern to account for state loyalty, the founders failed to
take party loyalty into account. Political parties arose almost
50   immediately after the Constitution was ratified. Problems with the
Electoral College quickly followed. In 1796, John Adams, a Federalist,
won the most electoral votes and became president. Thomas Jefferson, a
Democratic-Republican, was runner-up to Adams; he became the vice
president. Thus, the two top executives were bitter political rivals, an
55   unhappy and unintended state of affairs. In 1804, the Twelfth
Amendment stipulated that the Electoral College choose presidents and
vice presidents separately.

A more fundamental structural problem with the Electoral College
lay in the founders' anti-democratic intentions. As the nineteenth
60   century progressed, a wave of democratic reform swept Europe and the
United States. States began adopting direct popular election of a slate of
electors. Political parties began sponsoring their own slate of electors,
each of whom pledged to vote for their party's candidate in the Electoral
College. The result of each state's popular election began determining
65   which party's slate would take part in the Electoral College. This

democratization of the Electoral College had some unintended
consequences. First, since presidential elections were still determined
state-by-state by winner-take-all electoral votes, rather than by the
aggregate popular votes of all states, a candidate could lose the national
70   popular vote and still carry the Electoral College. Second, as party
divisions increased and the cost of presidential campaigns skyrocketed,
campaigns became increasingly focused on a few contested states, in
effect turning a national presidential election into a linked cluster of
local elections in which the interests of a few swing states determine
75   national policy decisions. Thus, the Electoral College has failed to fairly
balance state interests, as the founders had hoped, while remaining as
undemocratic as ever.

1.   The author's primary purpose in the passage is to

   (A) explain the workings of and reasoning behind an institution
        of the United States government
   (B) encourage protest over the fact that the most popular
        candidate did not win a recent election
   (C) summarize the history of the founders
   (D) confirm the efficacy of the presidential electoral process
   (E) criticize the founders for their distrust of democracy

2.   In lines 1–2, the author mentions that the 2000 election was the first
     time in 112 years that the candidate who won the popular vote did not
     become president because

   (A) the author wants the reader to understand that this was a
        freak occurrence and thus nothing deserving particular
        concern
   (B) the author wants to emphasize that elections follow
        patterns that can be traced over time
   (C) the author wants the reader to understand that this is a
        problem which has been able to go unnoticed for many
        years but which now demands our attention
   (D) the author wants the reader to realize that the American
        political scene in the twenty-first century will resemble
        that of the nineteenth century more than that of the
        twentieth century
   (E) the author wants the reader to recognize that elections held
        at the turn of the century are fundamentally different
        from those held in the middle of the century

3. In lines 9–10 the author writes, "the United States was to become a republic, not a democracy" to highlight the fact that

(A) the United States government was intended to approximate the government of Caesar's Roman Empire, not Ancient Greece

(B) the founders wanted the president to be elected by a select group of people, not the general population

(C) at the time, the Republican Party was much more powerful than the Democratic Party

(D) the founders wanted the electoral process to be open to the public

(E) the founders wanted to make sure that the government did not become a monarchy

4. In lines 12–16, the words "ignorant and unpropertied masses" serve to

(A) suggest that it was the founders' disdain for poorer and less educated Americans which made them steer away from a truly democratic system for presidential election

(B) articulate the author's distrust of people who did not go to college and do not own land

(C) argue for a direct correlation between education and professional success

(D) assert that, at the time the Electoral College was founded, most Americans were poor and undereducated

(E) argue that people who do not hold land and are not educated are all alike

5. Which of the following best expresses the point about the legislative branch of the government made in the third paragraph?

(A) The problems inherent in the legislative branch made it impossible for the Electoral College to offer a fair system.

(B) The legislative branch served as a model for the Electoral College in the way it attempted to balance the power of large and small states.

(C) The problems created by the Electoral College would be diffused by the balance of power established by the legislative branch.

(D) The system in place in the legislative branch made the plan for the Electoral college redundant.

(E) The system in place in the legislative branch necessitated the proposed organization of the Electoral College.

6. In lines 30–32, the statement that the candidate who received the most votes was elected, "as long as he had a majority of all votes cast," means that

    (A) a candidate would be elected president if he received more votes than anyone else
    (B) a candidate would only be elected president if he received a majority of the popular vote and a majority of the votes from the Electoral College
    (C) a candidate would only be voted president if he received a majority of the votes from the Electoral College and a majority of the votes from the Senate
    (D) a candidate would only be voted president if he received a majority of the votes from the Electoral College and a majority of the votes from the House of Representatives
    (E) if no candidate won more than half the votes, then no candidate would be elected

7. The purpose of the fifth paragraph is to

    (A) undermine the argument made thus far
    (B) convince the reader that the current practice of electing a president and vice president provides the best compromise
    (C) show how a well-intentioned system could lead to unexpected problems
    (D) summarize the points made so far
    (E) give evidence to support an argument offered in the fourth paragraph

8. In line 62, "slate" most nearly means

    (A) rock
    (B) schedule
    (C) tablet
    (D) covering
    (E) list

9. In stating that "as the nineteenth century progressed, a wave of
    democratic reform swept Europe and the United States" (lines 59–61),
    the writer assumes that

    (A) the individual states' adoptions of popular elections were
         part of a broader trend that spanned the Atlantic ocean
    (B) politicians in the United States wanted to be more like their
         European counterparts
    (C) politicians in Europe wanted to be more like their American
         counterparts
    (D) women would soon get to vote
    (E) the yearning for democracy that characterized the
         development of the American government originated in
         Europe

10. The author's statement in lines 67–70 that "a candidate could lose the
    national popular vote and still carry the Electoral College" depends on
    the fact that

    (A) a candidate who wins the popular vote in a certain state by
         even one vote still receives all of that state's Electoral
         College votes
    (B) electoral reforms put an end to the practice whereby a
         president from one party and a vice president from
         another party could be elected to serve together
    (C) voters in some states would not have their votes counted
         unless elections in other states resulted in a tie
    (D) incumbent presidents do not need to win a majority of the
         votes in order to retain office
    (E) the Electoral College is composed of the House of
         Representatives and the Senate

LONG READING PASSAGES: SOCIAL
SCIENCE—ANSWERS & EXPLANATIONS

1. **A**

The passage focuses on the way the Electoral College functions and the
logic that shaped its design. **B** is tempting because the fact that the most
popular candidate did not win the last election seems to be what motivated the author to write the passage, but the passage is focused on
explanation rather than protest—it is not until the final sentence that the
author expresses dissatisfaction with the electoral system. The passage

certainly does not praise the system, however, so **D** is incorrect. **C** and **E** are both incorrect because they offer details that are relevant to the passage but do not accurately represent its main focus.

2. **C**

Even though this question seems to focus on the passage's first sentence, the key to answering it correctly lies in understanding the passage's main idea. Obviously, the author would not have written the passage in the first place if he or she thought the phenomenon did not deserve our concern, so **A** is incorrect. The passage does not examine patterns, ways in which the twenty-first-century political scene will resemble that of the nineteenth century more than that of the twentieth century, or ways in which turn-of-the-century elections differ from mid-century elections, so **B**, **D**, and **E** are all incorrect. The author does seem to think that the potential for the Electoral College to select a candidate other than the one who won the popular vote is worthy of consideration, so **C** is the most logical answer.

3. **C**

The second paragraph focuses on the founders' distrust of democracy, or "mob rule" as they thought of it. Instead of a democracy they wanted a republic, in which the president was elected, but only by a small and select group of people. **E** is tempting, since a break with the tradition of monarchy was obviously an important factor in the establishment of the government, but this would have been equally the case if a democracy had been chosen from the beginning. **A** is incorrect because the fear of an American Caesar was uppermost in the founders' minds.

4. **A**

The words quoted in the question are more powerfully critical than the rest of the passage, and this alerts the reader to the fact that the author is articulating opinions held by somebody else, specifically the framers of the Electoral College, rather than expressing his or her own opinion (which makes all the other answers incorrect). The author uses such powerful language to suggest that it was the framers' disdainful prejudice against ordinary people's ability to make wise decisions that caused their distrust of democracy in principle, and which motivated them to create an electoral college rather than rely on a popular vote.

5.　**B**

Lines 17–25 explain that the Electoral College was designed to provide a balance of power between large and small states like that provided by the legislative branch of the government. The other answers are incorrect because they all suggest relationships between the Electoral College and the legislative branch not indicated in the passage.

6.　**E**

When talking about numbers, the word *majority* is used to refer to a number more than half of the total, so if a majority was required for election, that means that a candidate who received 49% of the votes would not be elected even if his nearest rival won only 45%. **A** is incorrect because it only explains the first half of the statement (that the candidate with the most votes would win). **B**, **C**, and **D** are incorrect because the statement only refers to votes in the Electoral College—the popular vote did not count, and presidential votes were only cast by the House of Representatives, if the Electoral College produced no majority.

7.　**C**

The first sentence of the fifth paragraph explains that the system the founders created to fairly balance the powers of the states did not anticipate the rise of political parties and the problems that this could cause in cases where the president and vice president were elected from different parties. **B** is tempting because it includes details from the paragraph, but nowhere does the author suggest that the current electoral system represents the best realistic option. **A**, **D**, and **E** do not accurately describe the paragraph.

8.　**E**

As used in line 62, "slate" is used to refer to the *list* of electors assembled by the political parties. None of the definitions offered by the other answers makes sense in the context of the sentence.

9.　**A**

The sentence quoted in the question precedes a statement about the states' adoptions of popular elections, implying that what happened in America was part of a trend that also manifested in Europe. There is no suggestion that this trend started on one side of the Atlantic or the other, however, so **B**, **C**, and **E** are all incorrect. No mention is made of women getting the vote, so **D** is incorrect as well.

10.   **A**

The key to answering this question correctly is to go back and read the sentence from which the quoted words were taken. Doing so reveals that a candidate can lose the aggregate, national popular vote but still win the presidency because of the "winner-take-all" nature of the Electoral College. A candidate receives all of a state's electoral votes even if he or she just barely wins that state's popular votes. Since the number of electoral votes is proportional to a state's population, a candidate can lose the national popular vote and yet win the presidency if he or she wins the popular vote by a hair in a few large states with many electoral votes but loses the popular vote by a landslide in many small states with few electoral votes. **B** offers information that is irrelevant to this phenomenon, and from an earlier paragraph. The other answers offer false statements not asserted in the passage.

SHORT READING PASSAGE: SCIENCE

Hurricanes are tropical storms with winds of over 75 miles per hour. They begin as thunderstorms that form over areas of the ocean where the water temperature exceeds 81 degrees Fahrenheit. The warmth and moisture in these regions provide the hurricane with its tremendous
5   power, which explains why hurricanes quickly weaken when they pass over cool water and dissipate soon after they hit land.

Although hurricanes themselves are only a real concern to coastal areas, they often give birth to tornadoes. These funnel clouds turn inland, leaving swaths of destruction in their wakes. Tornadoes destroy
10   power lines, damage homes and other property, and are responsible for dozens of deaths every year. These tragedies are becoming less common, however, as new weather technology makes it easier to predict the formation of tornadoes and provide early warning to the areas that may be affected.

1. Using its context in the passage, choose the word that best expresses the meaning of the term "dissipate," found in the final sentence of the first paragraph.

(A) intensify
(B) invert
(C) disappear
(D) reverse
(E) deplete

2.   What is the main purpose of the second paragraph?

(A) To convince the reader that hurricanes pose no threat to inland areas

(B) To explain in more detail the ideas introduced in the first paragraph

(C) To explain the most dangerous aspect of hurricanes

(D) To inform the reader why even people who live far from the ocean should be aware of hurricanes

(E) To assure the reader that the development of new early warning systems will render hurricanes harmless

SHORT READING PASSAGE: SCIENCE— ANSWERS & EXPLANATIONS

1.   C

The final sentence of the first paragraph explains that hurricanes draw their power from warmth and moisture, that they weaken in cold weather, and that they *dissipate* over dry land. If they draw their power from warmth and moisture, it seems likely that they would *disappear* over dry land, where moisture is mostly absent, so **C** is the correct answer. **A** is the opposite of the correct answer, and **E** does not make sense in the context of the sentence. **B** and **D** sound more plausible, but the passage does nothing to suggest that hurricanes *reverse* or *invert* over dry land (nor even what it would mean for them to do either of the these things), so **C** remains the best answer.

2.   D

The second paragraph states that hurricanes themselves only pose a direct threat to coastal areas, but also that they sometimes give rise to tornadoes, which can damage inland areas. Therefore, the paragraph provides a reason why even people who live far from the ocean should be aware of hurricanes— even if the hurricanes themselves won't reach inland, they may produce tornadoes, which very well could. **A** is incorrect because the paragraph only states that hurricanes pose no *direct* threat to inland areas, not that they pose no threat to inland areas at all. **B** is simply inaccurate. **C** is incorrect because the passage does not state or imply that tornadoes are the most dangerous aspect of hurricanes, only the most dangerous to inland areas. **E** is incorrect because the passage does not suggest that early warning systems will render hurricanes harmless, only that they will give people more time to prepare for tornadoes.

SHORT READING PASSAGE: SCIENCE

For thousands of years, people believed that owls were more like gods than animals. Even in modern times they have been used to signify wisdom, magic, and power, but the simple truth is that owls are no more divine than other birds. The large, round heads and huge, forward-
5   facing eyes that inclined ancient observers to believe that owls possessed divine intelligence are simply natural adaptations developed to help the predators catch the small animals that make up their food supply.

    Although owls do not possess any of the mystical powers often
10 attributed to them in mythology, they are formidable hunters whose skill surpasses that of other birds of prey. Their acute senses ensure that owls rarely fail to notice a potential meal, and their ability to fly silently means that the unfortunate mouse identified by the owl as its next snack never realizes it is the object of an attack until too late.

1.   In the second sentence of the first paragraph, the word "signify" means

    (A) denote
    (B) magnify
    (C) make important
    (D) insult
    (E) predict

2.   The last sentence of the first paragraph provides

    (A) a summary of the facts presented earlier
    (B) an example to prove a controversial theory presented earlier
    (C) an explanation that rebuts a misconception presented
        earlier
    (D) an assertion that will be proved later on
    (E) a view that will be contradicted later on

3.   The purpose of the passage as a whole is to

(A) assure the reader that owls are no different from other birds

(B) persuade the reader that owls had an important place in ancient mythology

(C) assert that while owls are not magical they are extraordinary in other ways

(D) defend an attitude that has recently come under attack

(E) discredit an idea that has been gaining in popularity

SHORT READING PASSAGE: SCIENCE— ANSWERS & EXPLANATIONS

1.   A

Reading the whole sentence, it is clear that *signify* must mean "stand for" or "represent." The word among the answer choices which has the closest meaning is *denote*. None of the other words in the answer choices comes so close to the apparent meaning of the word in the passage.

2.   C

The final sentence of the first paragraph explains that those features of the owl's physiognomy that suggest divine intelligence are really just natural adaptations evolved to help them be more successful hunters. This explanation rebuts the misconception presented at the start of the paragraph that owls are more like gods than humans. None of the other answers offers an accurate description of the sentence.

3.   C

The first paragraph deflates the notion that owls are supernatural creatures, but the second half explains that they are exceptionally well-evolved as hunters. **A** is incorrect because the passage makes it clear that owls possess traits not shared with other birds. **B** is incorrect because the passage states the prominence of owls in mythology as a matter of fact, not something of which the reader needs to be persuaded. **D** and **E** are incorrect because the passage does not suggest that any of the ideas or attitudes it covers have become more popular or come under attack. It discredits the idea that owls are magical, but this idea is not shown to be gaining in popularity.

SHORT READING PASSAGE: HUMANITIES

One of the features that distinguish traditional Pueblo pottery from other types of clay art is the absence of machinery from all parts of the creative process. The clay is gathered, processed, and finally shaped by hand. Instead of using a potter's wheel to create vases and other round objects, the Pueblo pottery artist rolls clay into long pieces and then painstakingly coils them into layers of circles. Paints are produced from plants and minerals found near the Pueblo village and applied with a handmade brush fashioned from a yucca cactus.

This adherence to tradition is one of the things that make Pueblo pottery so attractive to the art collector. Since the Pueblo potter shuns techniques of mass production, the collector can be sure that every piece of Pueblo clay art is uniquely shaped. This quality also makes examples of Pueblo pottery excellent gifts.

1. According to information provided in the passage, what change to the Pueblo pottery production process would do most to make examples of Pueblo pottery LESS attractive as gifts?

   (A) Substitution of synthetic paints for the natural pigments currently used
   (B) Changes to the way the clay is gathered and processed
   (C) Changes to the type of clay used
   (D) The replacement of traditional Pueblo decoration with more modern designs
   (E) The introduction of molds to guarantee uniform size and shape

2.   The function of the first paragraph is to

   (A) establish a thesis that will be refuted in the second
        paragraph
   (B) establish a thesis that will be supported in the second
        paragraph
   (C) provide information that will be used to explain a
        phenomenon discussed in the second paragraph
   (D) present two differing opinions about Pueblo pottery
   (E) explain why it is important for people interested in
        collecting art to learn about Pueblo pottery

3.   According to information provided in the passage, what change would
     do MOST to threaten future production of traditional Pueblo pottery?

   (A) The replacement of the traditional process with
        standardized technology
   (B) The increase in popularity of Pueblo pottery
   (C) A loss in interest in Pueblo pottery on the part of art
        collectors
   (D) A reduction in the number of Pueblo pottery pieces given as
        gifts each year
   (E) The introduction of new styles of pottery similar to Pueblo
        pottery

SHORT READING PASSAGE: HUMANITIES— ANSWERS & EXPLANATIONS

1.   E

The last sentence of the passage asserts that it is the uniqueness of
Pueblo pottery pieces that makes them attractive as gifts. If molds were
introduced to the production process to guarantee uniform size and
shape, this uniqueness would be lost, and pieces of Pueblo pottery would
be less attractive as gifts. **A** and **D** are tempting since they propose changes
that would seem likely to make Pueblo pottery more "modern" and thus
possibly less attractive for gift-giving, but the passage connects the artwork's
popularity among gift-givers to the unique shape of each piece.

2.   C

The first paragraph explains how each piece of Pueblo pottery is shaped
and painted by hand. This explains the uniqueness of Pueblo pottery,

which is the focus of the second paragraph. None of the other answer choices presents an accurate description of the first paragraph.

3.   A

Pueblo pottery is defined by its hand-wrought nature. The introduction of standardized technology would threaten the production of *traditional* Pueblo pottery. The changes proposed in **B, C, D**, and **E** might all reduce demand for Pueblo pottery, but this would not necessarily threaten production (there is no suggestion that the primary motivation for production of Pueblo pottery is commercial).

PAIRED READING PASSAGE: HUMANITIES

Directions: *The passages below are followed by questions based on the content of the passages and the relationship between the two passages. Answer the questions on the basis of what the passage* states *or* implies *and on any introductory material provided.*

Questions 1–10 refer to the following pair of passages.

These passages, adapted from recently published articles, discuss restoring acknowledged masterpieces of art. The first passage is written by a renowned professor of art history. The second is written by a journalist.

Passage 1

Watch reruns of so-called historical dramas on television, and you will have little difficulty in identifying the decade in which the show was originally produced. Does anybody really believe that the long-running 1970s television show *Little House on the Prairie* actually provided an
5   accurate glimpse of nineteenth-century rural life? The actor who played "Pa," for instance, lacked a beard, even though men of that period generally had facial hair. His feathered hair and perfect white teeth further located the show in the 1970s and detracted from the authenticity of the show's intended reconstruction of a bygone era. No
10 one expects the entertainment industry to accurately characterize the past for its own sake; shows like *Little House* use an imagined past to satisfy a nostalgic urge for a way of life that never existed. It is only to be expected that *Little House* says far more about the time in which it was

created than the time in which it was set, and one should not get too
15 worked up about it. However, the contemporary trend of restoring
classic works of art raises similar issues in a far more serious context.

Restoration, as the word itself implies, assumes that one can recreate
an artist's original intent and product. At best, restorers' and museum
directors' aesthetic preferences and historical theories drive
20 restorations, for it is impossible to step outside one's historical context.
How can restorers be so sure that removing a layer of lacquer isn't
merely their subconscious attempt to refashion an artwork according to
contemporary tastes? What's "restorative" about that? The "restored"
Sistine Chapel may look "authentic" today, but will it still look so when
25 aesthetic and historical theories have changed? Will the newly bright
colors heralded as the master's work reborn look as embarrassingly
anachronistic as *Little House*? Surely the best approach with any great
work of art is to simply leave it alone.

Restorers use the science that informs their task to lend an
30 unwarranted objectivity to their activities. Science's objectivity is beside
the point. A scientist can determine the molecular composition of the
substances that make up a painting, but a scientist cannot determine
the original intent and state of the artist. It will be the art-historian
restorer who will use that objective data to decide which substances to
35 remove. The art historian will use his at least partially subjective
judgment, informed by objective scientific data though it may be, to
deem which substances are authentically original. The crux of the
problem is that restoration assumes that a contemporary art historian
can reproduce the original artwork by recreating the often subconscious
40 decisions of the original artist.

Of course there are occasions in which an artwork must be restored,
but only when the work's existence is threatened. But why have so many
works of art that are not facing an imminent threat been restored? The
reasons, sadly, are more a matter of marketing than conservation. The
45 recent exhortations to clean up Michelangelo's David provide a good
example. The Galleria dell'Accademia wanted to spruce David up for his
five-hundredth birthday, for they knew that a refurbished David would
be catnip for tourists and a windfall for the museum. Not only ticket
sales and food concessions but also the inevitable T-shirts, posters, and
50 other cross-marketed products would fill their coffers. Profit, then, and
not restoration, is the true cause of the art-restoration craze. Like their
Medici forerunners, museum directors' love of art rarely outstrips their
love of money.

Passage 2

55 After years of hand-wringing, the verdict followed hard on the heels of
the unveiling: Michelangelo's David was once again revealed to be the
most beautiful representation of the male form ever sculpted. The art
world was greatly relieved. In fact, David had not been restored, but
merely cleaned, which had been the museum director's intent. Free from
blemishes and stains, that statue again revealed its essential
60 seamlessness. Lines flowed without interruption; shapes melted
imperceptibly into one another.

As is usually the case with restorations, controversy had plagued the
project, and understandably so. The sad history of poorly restored
masterworks has tainted all restorative efforts and prejudiced much of
65 the art world. But the hysteria that surrounded David's restoration was
excessive. Chief among the concerns was a debate over the cleaning
method. The original restorer wanted to use "dry" techniques to rub off
the dirt. When a rival "wet" technique was chosen, he resigned in a huff,
convinced that any application of water to the marble would
70 permanently damage the sculpture. His replacement mixed cellulose,
clay, and water and wrapped the creamy ointment in rice paper. This
compress was then held against the stone, which lifted grime from the
surface. This arrangement ensured that only distilled water had any
contact with the sculpture.

75 The recent change in David's appearance was neither the first nor the
most intrusive. Far from it: in 1504, an angry mob expressed their
political dissent by throwing stones at the statue. David's left arm was
broken into three pieces only 23 years later. In the mid-nineteenth
century, David was moved from the Piazza della Signoria courtyard,
80 where he had stood exposed to the elements for over 350 years, to his
present home, the Galleria dell'Accademia. Well-meaning restorers then
gave David an acid bath to remove centuries of accumulated pigeon
droppings. In 1991, a deranged tourist attacked David's toe with a
hammer. Despite this long history, or perhaps because of it, many
85 scholars are loath to make even the slightest change to David's frame.

It is worth noting, however, that the recent cleaning uncovered a
crack on David's left ankle. David's real enemy is not sophisticated,
respectful, and painstaking cleaning, but an earthquake—a relatively
common event in Italy. Scientists are working now to determine how
90 best to protect David from such an event. In the end, the restoration
that so many feared may well have given us the impetus to combat a far
more dangerous threat to this great sculpture.

1. In the context of lines 21–23 of Passage 1, the reference to "subconscious attempt" refers to

    (A) an actor's inability to portray the time in which he lives
    (B) a museum director's questionable motives in organizing a restoration project
    (C) a restorer's tendency to favor the aesthetics of his time
    (D) an artist's unique ability to recreate the past on canvas
    (E) a funder's secret motive in donating to a restoration project

2. The word "anachronistic" is used in lines 25–27 to signify

    (A) something that is very old
    (B) strong optimism
    (C) something out of place in its time
    (D) peers who share a similar agenda
    (E) color that is bright and flashy in nature

3. The argument that the desire for profit drives restoration projects in lines 49–52 would be most STRENGTHENED by which of the following?

    (A) Museum directors have openly stated that profit was the primary motivating factor in initiating restoration projects
    (B) No museum restoration project has ever turned a profit
    (C) Many art pieces are difficult to represent on T-shirts and mugs
    (D) Most art restoration projects are undertaken on pieces that are on the verge of disintegration, regardless of the popularity of those pieces
    (E) Museums never display restored works of art to the public

4. According to the author of Passage 2, those who argued that the David should not be cleaned were

    (A) reasonably prudent
    (B) unnecessarily redundant
    (C) overly emotional
    (D) highly biased
    (E) unforgivably ignorant

5. The word "tainted" in lines 64 most nearly means

   (A) physically putrefied
   (B) morally corrupted
   (C) intrinsically weakened
   (D) inappropriately pigmented
   (E) adversely colored

6. According to Passage 2, opponents of David's restoration failed to take into account that

   (A) David has been restored without ill effect several times in the past five hundred years
   (B) we do not know how Michelangelo would have felt about the restoration
   (C) water might damage the surface of the sculpture
   (D) the current David has withstood many and more severe changes since his original creation
   (E) there is a copy of the original David standing in the Piazza della Signoria courtyard

7. Which of the following most accurately describes the organization of the last paragraph of Passage 2?

   (A) The author provides a counterexample that forces him to alter his argument.
   (B) The author relates an unforeseen benefit of an event he has supported.
   (C) The author makes a prediction of future events.
   (D) The author reiterates the argument against his point of view.
   (E) The author supports his position with historical evidence.

8. Both passages are primarily concerned with

   (A) the successful cleaning of David
   (B) the Sistine Chapel's restoration
   (C) the inadvisability of cleaning paintings with water
   (D) the best way to depict the past on television
   (E) the appropriateness of art restoration

9. The author of Passage 2 would most likely respond to the author of Passage 1's argument that profit drives restorations (lines 49–52) by doing which of the following?

(A) Denying that profit ever motivates restoration projects

(B) Maintaining that it is possible to accurately recreate the original artwork through restoration

(C) Arguing that even if profit motivates restorations, it still ends up preserving and popularizing beautiful and enriching works of art

(D) Insisting that scientific research, not profit, motivates restoration projects

(E) Refuting the notion that art historians can be objective

10. How would the author of Passage 1 most likely respond to the author of Passage 2's report that "the recent cleaning uncovered a crack on David's left ankle" (lines 86–87)?

(A) The restoration caused the crack.

(B) The crack will cut into the museum's projected profits, as visitors will be disappointed.

(C) Since contemporary restorers can't recreate the original intent of the artist whose work they restore, we can't be sure that Michelangelo didn't intend for that crack to be there.

(D) Water caused the crack; the "dry" method should have been used after all.

(E) Further restoration work should begin immediately, as the artwork's existence is threatened.

PAIRED READING PASSAGE: HUMANITIES— ANSWERS & EXPLANATIONS

1.   **C**

In lines 17–28 the author discusses his concern that art restorers have a tendency to restore pieces according to the tastes of their time. He uses the Sistine Chapel as an example. The frescoes have been restored and are now very bright, but the author fears that this brightness reflects contemporary taste, and not necessarily the author's original intention. In other words, an art restorer might "subconsciously" be making an "attempt" to restore a piece under the influence of modern tastes.

2.   C

This is a vocabulary-in-context question. To answer this question, first take a look at the sentence in which the word "anachronistic" is used. The author writes: "Will the newly bright colors heralded as the master's work reborn look as embarrassingly anachronistic as *Little House*?" In this part of the passage, the author is making the case that art restorers cannot escape the aesthetic and historical theories of their time. Notice the comparison to reruns of *Little House on the Prairie*. Remember, at the beginning of the passage, the author made the point that even though *Little House* is supposed to take place in the nineteenth century, it has a lot of features of the 1970s. In other words, elements of the show look out of place considering the intended temporal setting, the nineteenth century. *Anachronistic* means exactly this: *ana* means "back" or "backwards"; *chron* means "time." Choice **A** does not quite work. We are looking for a word that specifically addresses things that are erroneously placed in an incorrect temporal setting, not old things. Choice **B** does not fit the tone of the sentence; do the words "suspicion" and "optimism" really go together? You might have been tempted by choice **D** if you thought that the root *chron* in *anachronistic* is related to a "crony," or a peer. But this definition does not fit the context of the sentence. Similarly, you might have been attracted to choice **E** because it mentions "color," but remember, root *chron* means "time." The root *chrom* relates to color, as in "chromatic."

3.   A

The author of Passage 1 claims in the final paragraph that profit, not preservation, drives museum directors' initiation of restoration projects. If museum directors came right out and said that profit drives their decision to restore great works of art, that would greatly strengthen the author's argument. Choice **B** may be tempting because it mentions the word *profit*. But it's a distortion—surely, if restoration projects of famous works of art tend not to realize a profit, then their continued occurrence cannot be ascribed to the profit motive! Choice **C** also doesn't strengthen the argument. The author argued that some of the profits of restored artworks comes from reproductions of the newly refurbished image on T-shirts and mugs. If this were difficult to do, for whatever reason, in many cases, that certainly would lower potential profit. Choice **D** actually does not strengthen the author's argument. If it were true that most restoration projects were conducted to prevent the imminent destruction of a piece of art, regardless of its popularity, then profit might not be the primary motivating factor, as the author claims. Finally, if museums never displayed restored artworks, that surely would undermine the author's argument that profit drives restoration projects—it certainly wouldn't *strengthen* that argument. Therefore, **E** is incorrect.

4.   **C**

In the second paragraph of Passage 2, the author states: "But the hysteria that surrounded David's restoration was excessive." In other words, the author feels that critics were too emotional, or "hysterical." Even if *hysteria* is meant figuratively—and we can't be sure that it isn't meant literally—the conclusion still holds: the author thinks that the critics were far too emotional about the restoration. Furthermore, the original restorer resigned "in a huff," which means, "under the influence of an often-passing burst of self-righteous anger or resentment." Since this is the author's position, he would not agree with choice **A**, as he didn't think the anti-restorationists were being reasonably prudent, or "showing wisdom and good judgment disciplined by reason." Choice **B** is the "left-field" choice—*redundant* means "repetitive." In any ongoing debate, positions will be repeated; this choice distorts that unavoidable fact of debate. Furthermore, the author never mentions redundancy as a fault of the anti-preservationists. You may have been tempted by choice **D** because *biased* is a negative word meaning "unreasonably prejudiced." However, the author's complaint is not about the anti-preservationists' bias, but about the level of emotion with which they pushed their view. One can be biased without being hysterical; one can very calmly state a biased opinion. Choice **E** is also tricky. It's clear that the author thought the anti-preservationists were wrong, but this is far too extreme a description of the author's tone. They weren't *unforgivably* wrong—the entire third paragraph explains why well-meaning people might be reticent about messing around with David after years of abuse. Moreover, there is no evidence that the anti-preservationists were *ignorant*, either. The original restorer, it's safe to infer, was not ignorant; he was merely wrong in this case.

5.   **E**

This is a tough vocabulary-in-context question. The sentence in question is: "The sad history of poorly restored masterworks has tainted all restorative efforts and prejudiced much of the art world." *Tainted* has many meanings—as do most words in VIC stems. Which applies here? If you take out *tainted*, the idea is that the history of botched restorations has given restoration a bad name. Which choice matches this? Choices **A**, **B**, and **C**—all legitimate meanings of *tainted*, don't match. Choice **D** is a nasty distractor. The passage is about restoring paintings—and this part of the passage is specifically about how botched restorations have prejudiced much of the art world against restorations. So, you might lunge at **D**, thinking that prior restorers had often used an inappropriate pigment. But you'd have been fooled. Despite the seeming similarity of **D**'s *pigmented* and **E**'s *colored*, the sense of the latter is not literal but figurative. The history of botched restorations has prejudiced many in the art world—has *adversely colored* those people's opinion of all restoration projects.

6.   D

The author devotes the third paragraph to the violent indignities that David has suffered for half a millennium to show how relatively benevolent and helpful the restoration project was. (What's a gentle cleaning next to stone-throwing or crazed hammering?) Choice **A** is a distortion: we're told of only one restoration—that occurred in the nineteenth century when the statue was bathed in acid. It's unlikely that the author would point to that event as support for his position—in fact, the concluding sentence of the third paragraph acknowledges that the long history of relatively violent assaults on David probably explains some scholars' extreme reticence to cause any further damage, however well-intentioned. **B** is the left-field choice. Nothing is said about what Michelangelo would have thought about the entire issue. **C** is the exact opposite of what you're looking for—the fear of applying water to the sculpture is what made the first restorer walk off the job! And **E** is a distortion. No one cares about a replica of David, no matter where it stands. Everyone was concerned with what to do with the original. Furthermore, according to the passage, the original David was moved from that Piazza della Signoria 150 years ago.

7.   B

In conclusion, the author notes that despite all the hoopla over David's restoration, the process actually uncovered a far more dangerous threat to the statue: a crack that might cause the statue to crumble during one of Italy's frequent earthquakes. (This is a good example of irony, by the way.) Far from being a counterexample that forces the author to modify his argument, as **A** claims, this unforeseen benefit of David's restoration supports the careful and respectful restoration of great works of art. **C** is incorrect because no actual prediction is made. We're told that scientists are *presently* working on the earthquake problem, which is a potential threat that lies in the *future*. But no specific prediction is made. Even the statement that earthquakes are common in Italy is a historical statement, not a prediction about the future: they've happened in the past; they may happen again in the future. But we can't be sure. The author does not restate counterarguments, as **D** claims, nor does he support his main idea—that the David restoration was a worthwhile undertaking that did not warrant the hysterical reaction of many in the art world—with any historical data. So, **E** is incorrect.

8. **E**

This is the main idea/purpose item. Both passages discuss art restoration, sharing the cleaning of David as a common subject. But while the author of Passage 2 considers the cleaning of David a success, the author of Passage 1, while not commenting on the advisability or success of the venture, uses David's restoration to make a point about how profit, not preservation, motivates restoration projects. Furthermore, the author of Passage 1 mentions David only at the end of the passage; it's not his primary concern. This means that choice **A** cannot be correct. The author of Passage 2 never mentions the Sistine Chapel; this is mentioned only in Passage 1. The author of Passage 2 mentions one restorer's opinion that cleaning *sculptures* with water is inadvisable; the author of Passage 1 does not discuss water as a restorative agent at all. Eliminate choice **C**. The author of Passage 1 mentions television in the first paragraph as an introduction to his discussion about how attainable historical authenticity is, but the author of passage 2 never mentions television at all. The correct choice is **E**, as both authors are chiefly concerned with art restoration.

9. **C**

Items such as these require you to "get inside the head" of the authors. If you were the author of Passage 2, what would you think about the author of Passage 1's argument? Luckily, the SAT usually gives you a distillation of the particular argument (*that profit drives restorations*) and a line reference. Keep in mind tone and the unlikelihood that extreme answers can be correct when checking out the answer choices. **A** seems a bit extreme. Would the author of Passage 2 be so naïve as to deny that profit *ever* plays a role in restoration projects? Unlikely; eliminate. **B** is a distortion. Sure, the author of Passage 1 spends some time arguing that accurate recreation of the original artwork is impossible. But that's not the argument this item is about, nor do we have any evidence of what the author of Passage 2 would think of that argument. **C** seems to be the *most likely* response. The author of Passage 2 spoke of the restored David in glowing, positive terms. His concern about the threat earthquakes may pose to David further reinforces his clear love of the artwork. It's reasonable to infer that this author would feel that the author of Passage 1 is being a bit too purist. One can imagine the author of Passage 2 saying, "If profit motivates the restoration of works like David, then let's hear it for the profit motive! I'm far more concerned with preserving great works of art, no matter where the money comes from." **D** distorts things quite tortuously. The item asks about profit motive—science isn't mentioned. Furthermore, neither author argues that scientific research in and of itself is driving restoration projects. In both passages, science provides tools for the restorers. **E** repeats the distortion of **B**—this item is about profit driving restoration, not about the essential subjectivity of art historians—but with a further twist. The author of Passage 1 argues that art historians *can't* be objective. So the author of Passage 2 can hardly refute something that the author of Passage 1 doesn't maintain at all! Eliminate this choice.

10.   **E**

Again, you have to "role-play" here; you're now the author of Passage 1. You've just been told about the crack in David's ankle. How would you *most likely* respond? **A** seems very unlikely. The author of Passage 1 doesn't challenge the efficacy of restoration—he merely doubts that it occurs for reasons of conservation rather than profit. This distractor tries to mix the author of Passage 1 with the anti-restorationists in Passage 2. Always keep your "actors" straight in Reading Passages. Choice **B** superficially refers to the profit-motivation that the author of Passage 1 believes drives restoration projects. But this is hardly a likely reaction to the discovery of the crack itself, and it contains a very shaky inference: that visitors will be so disappointed they won't come to see the famous statue. First, we don't know how big or noticeable the crack is. Second, we don't know that visitors won't rush in even larger droves, worried that David may not be long for this world. Reject the choice. **C** is a distortion. Again, the author of Passage 1 does maintain that contemporary preservationists cannot read the minds of dead artists whose work they restore, but it strains credulity to picture the author of Passage 1, who seems a reasonable, if opinionated person (tone is all-important, remember) seriously maintaining that Michelangelo purposely included an imperfection in his statue! Like **A**, **D** tries to confuse the test-taker by conflating the author of Passage 1, who has nothing to say about "wet" versus "dry" restoration techniques, with the original restorer, who quit when his "dry" technique was rejected. The author of Passage 1's main points were about the impossibility of recapturing original artistic intent and the motivation of profit in restoration projects. Choice **E** is supported by Passage 1: the author states that the only occasion for restorative intervention is in the face of an imminent threat. The potential for an earthquake to destroy an already cracked David would most likely engender this reaction from the author of Passage 1.

ABOUT THE AUTHOR

Doug Tarnopol brings a unique mix of talents and experience to SparkNotes and the New SAT *Power Tactics* series. He has taught and tutored students of all backgrounds and advised both students and parents on preparing for the SAT. Doug graduated magna cum laude from Cornell University in 1992, earning a B.A. in History. He continued his work in the history and sociology of science at the University of Pennsylvania, receiving an M.A. in 1996.

While in graduate school, Doug began teaching SAT test-prep classes. After completing his graduate work, Doug moved to New York City and continued working in test prep, adding PSAT, SCI HI, SAT II: Writing, SAT II: Math, GMAT, and other courses to his repertoire. In 1999, Doug became a curriculum developer, designing instructional material for state proficiency exams.

Doug also writes fiction and poetry. He is an avid drummer, biker, and reader. He currently lives in Metuchen, New Jersey.

SPARKNOTES
Power Tactics for the New SAT

The Critical Reading Section

Reading Passages
Sentence Completions

The Math Section

Algebra
Data Analysis, Statistics & Probability
Geometry
Numbers & Operations

The Writing Section

The Essay
*Multiple Choice Questions: Identifying Sentence Errors,
Improving Sentences, Improving Paragraphs*

The New SAT

Test-Taking Strategies
Vocabulary Builder